Praise for *Yemaya*

"Raven Morgaine is a gifted storyteller and visionary in multiple disciplines. His jam-packed, beautifully illustrated book will lead you to understand, in laymen's terms, anything and everything you ever wanted to know about the African orisha, Yemaya, as a noninitiate. This book is an enveloping and compelling read. It will lead you to take meaningful action, following in Morgaine's footsteps, to immerse yourself in Yemaya's complex energies."

—Stephanie Rose Bird, author of *Sticks, Stones, Roots, and Bones* and *365 Days of Hoodoo*

"Not only a beautiful offering to Yemaya herself, Raven Morgaine's *Yemaya: Orisha, Goddess, and Queen of the Sea* is also a much-needed guide for those interested in respectfully honoring her. Filled with fluid stories, personal experiences, history, song, prayers, herbal knowledge, and more, this is a must-have for any water witch interested in honoring the radiant Goddess of the Sea."

—Annwyn Avalon, author of *The Way of the Water Priestess* and *Water Witchcraft*

"*Yemaya* is a supremely well-written, engaging, and all-encompassing account of the goddess and her many attributes and paths. It includes real-life stories depicting the love that Yemaya has for humanity and the many miracles she has performed. Raven Morgaine has the grasp of Santeria, as did my Cuban elders, and his stunning artwork dedicated to Yemaya is breathtaking! Written for neophytes as well as seasoned *santeros*, this is a captivating tribute to Yemaya and destined to become a classic."

—Miss Aida, *santera* and author of *Hoodoo Cleansing and Protection Magic* and *Hoodoo Justice Magic*

"What an amazing tribute to the goddess to whom I have
been crowned for so many years. This homage to Yemaya will
resonate with and enlighten any reader. Raven Morgaine delivers
authenticity to the *pataki* or parables that represents the African
diaspora in its truest form. *Yemaya* is stellar literature."

> —Alexander Cabot, santero, high priest,
> and author of *Touched by the Goddess*

"Yemaya is a dedicated mother, powerful goddess, ruthless
warrior, possessive lover, wise healer, and among the oldest deities
in Africa. Venerated in numerous magical traditions and religions
around the globe, her origin is so uncertain that it is quite easy
to think of Yemaya as the first Mother Goddess of Africa, even
perhaps as the first Mother Goddess of humanity, as, in the end,
we all come from Africa, and, in one way or another, we all
descend from her. In his book, *Yemaya*, Raven Morgaine guides you
through Yemaya's myths and *pataki* and evokes her in her highest
splendor. For followers of the Yoruba religion, Lucumi, Umbanda,
Candomblé, and Santeria, as well as the many paths of modern
Vodou, this book is a pivotal tool."

> —Elhoim Leafar, author of *The Magical Art of Crafting
> Charm Bags* and *Manifestation Magic*

YEMAYA

*Orisha, Goddess,
and Queen of the Sea*

RAVEN MORGAINE

WEISER BOOKS

This edition first published in 2021 by Weiser Books, an imprint of
Red Wheel/Weiser, LLC
With offices at:
65 Parker Street, Suite 7
Newburyport, MA 01950
www.redwheelweiser.com

ISBN: 978-1-57863-743-0

Library of Congress Cataloging-in-Publication Data available upon request.

Cover design by Kathryn Sky-Peck
Cover illustration © Bernadett Bagyinka
Interior photos/images by Raven Morgaine
Interior by Deborah Dutton
Typeset in Adobe Garamond and Frutiger LT Std
Printed in the United States of America
IBI

10 9 8 7 6 5 4 3 2 1

This book is dedicated to my late baby sister, Kristina, the little mermaid. You were the very best of humanity, even at your worst. All my love forever.

TABLE OF CONTENTS

In the Beginning

As human beings, we have always sought to give faces and names to the natural and spiritual forces we encounter in order to understand and relate to them, to make them more personal, and to render them less frightening. In Yoruban tradition, these forces are known as *orishas*. Orishas are not gods or goddesses, in the Western sense. They are more like archangels or higher spirits—intermediaries between mankind and the transcendant forces of the universe. In the mythos of Yorubaland, a region in West Africa that encompasses western and southwestern Nigeria, Benin, Ghana, Togo, and the Gulf of Guinea, the orishas were brought into being by a supreme creator named Olodumare. Since this region is home to many rivers—including the Oba, the Ogun, the Ogunpa, the Omi Osun, the Osun, the Otin, and the Oueme—rivers in particular, and water in general, came to play a large role in the spiritual traditions of the region. Indeed, many Yoruban orishas, including Yemaya, were originally river spirits.

After Olodumare created the earth, gathering up all the dust and particles of matter in the universe, he created a vast hole into which he poured the remaining gasses accumulated during the creation of the planet, forming the first ocean. Immediately, a dark figure arose from the deepest depths, swimming in increasingly rapid circles until it breeched the surface of the water and emerged shining and magnificent. The figure was humanoid from head to waist, with the tail of a great sea serpent. As the spray of the ocean waters hung in the air around it, the figure proclaimed: "I am Olokun, owner of the depths, of the waters." He then dove back beneath the sea and vanished into the darkness.

As the ocean spray brought forth by Olokun evaporated, it began to rain. When this rain touched the salt water, the spirit Yembo appeared, radiant and regal, glittering with sea salt and clothed in a gown of flowing water. "I am Yembo," she cried. "Where the light of sun and moon penetrate the water, there is my kingdom to be found."

Yembo is traditionally seen as the first incarnation of Yemaya, the intriguing oceanic Mother of All life. Few spirits are more beloved, adopted, co-opted, and assimilated than this one. She appears in many different faiths and is called by many different variations of her full name—*Ye Omo Eja*, "the mother whose children are as numerous as the fish." In West Africa, she evolved into the goddess Yemaya, whose appearance as Yembo heralded the beginning of the time of the orishas on earth. Many believe that the sojourn of the orishas here will end when hers does. In many traditions, she is considered to have given birth to the first fourteen orishas, as well as to the first humans and the sun and the moon. She brought the power of procreation into the world, becoming the patroness of pregnant woman and their children, both born and unborn.

After emerging as a West African river goddess, Yemaya left Africa to travel with her children in overcrowded slave ships during the Middle Passage—the transportation of enslaved Africans across the Atlantic Ocean to the Americas that began in 1518 and continued into the mid-19th century—to try to protect them from the horrors to come. She and the orisha Oshun traveled with them across the seas wrapped in the rain in order to watch over them and succor them in their pain and despair. Indeed, so great is Yemaya's love for her children that no matter where they set foot, no matter how strange or foreign the land, she remains with them to guide and protect them.

As her praise and worship spread throughout the world, Yemaya's role expanded and she took control over all the waters of the world—salt water, fresh water (which she shares with her spiritual sister, Oshun, who is sometimes also considered to be her daughter), and the rain that falls from the heavens. She reigns over the water of our bodies—our sweat, our tears, and the amniotic fluids of the womb. Even our blood belongs to her. She is the Thrice-Crowned Queen of earth, sea, and moon.

Yemaya is often depicted as a twin-tailed siren, the link between the conscious and the subconscious, the solid and the liquid. Because of her dominion over the unfathomable depths of the human psyche, her influence is primarily felt on an inner level, but manifests on the physical plane as well. Once we have connected with her, she is truly always with us—inside us, guiding and healing us. Like all mothers, she sees and expects the best in and from us, pushing us to live the best lives we can as the best versions of ourselves. She knows our full potential and does not like to see us squander that potential in pursuit of meaningless goals, bad habits, and laziness. Yemaya works to manifest her own goals twenty-four hours a day and, while she does not expect that from us, she does expect an honest daily effort to strive toward and grow into our full capacity.

Yemaya changes form as she travels the world through the rain. In Egypt, she trades fins for feathers and becomes Isis. In Haiti, she becomes a lunar goddess. In Brazil, she becomes the country's patron saint. And so, from the cradle of all life, the Ocean Mother spreads her influence wherever living waters flow.

Aspects of the Goddess

To truly call upon Yemaya's power over the primordial forces of nature requires an appreciation of her many aspects and knowledge of a distinct set of doctrines and practices that need to be addressed in order to build a relationship with her. (Not to mention the role that Eleggua plays in this process, which we will discuss in chapter 7.) An in-depth understanding of these is essential if your goal is to blend the Mother of All Life and her court of sirens and water spirits into your spiritual practice successfully. Only when you have achieved an understanding of Yemaya's aspects will you be able to call on her to help you as you continue along your soul's journey.

It is important to note here that the many aspects of Yemaya are said to exist all at once, yet individually, and are often referred to as her "sisters." These sisters are considered to be the royal spiritual family of the sea.

On the whole, modern Pagan practitioners who have adopted the worship and veneration of Yemaya see her only as the archetypal patient, compassionate, and loving Mother. But she plays far more than that one role. As you will see in the coming chapters, she is also lover, witch, magician, warrior, and scourge, and there is much more to this extremely complicated goddess than most outsiders acknowledge. Hopefully, this book will give you insight into Yemaya's other roles, aspects, incarnations, and paths. To fully comprehend her complexity, you must know that all of her paths reflect a process of reincarnation that occurs after a series of spiritual and impactful events that cause her to be reborn, and her prior incarnation to ascend onto a higher spiritual plane.

Simply incorporating Yemaya into your spiritual practice does not make you one of her priests or priestesses, however. Nor does it make you her child in the way that these terms are used in African

Traditional Religions. These titles cannot belong to those who are complete outsiders to these traditions until they have gone through years of strict and rigorous study and have been initiated by a consecrated priest or priestess of the tradition. But anyone can become a student or devotee of Yemaya and incorporate her into their spiritual practices. This book is intended to help you reunite with the Mother of All Life and the siren of our dreams.

What this book is absolutely *not* intended to be is a book about the practice of African Traditional Religions. This is *not* a book about the practice of Ifa, or Santeria, or Candomblé, or any of the other traditional African practices brought to the New World during the Middle Passage. Nor is it a book on how to practice any religion other than your own, simply incorporating Yemaya into that existing belief system, whether it be Christianity, or Wicca, or witchcraft, or any other Pagan tradition. It is true that some Christian beliefs can be seen as associated with Yemaya through sacred figures like the Blessed Mother, the Stella Maris ("Star of the Sea," a title also associated with Isis), or Our Lady of Regla, the Black Madonna with whom Yemaya is often identified. But this association does not reflect a true appreciation of her powers. It is true, however, that *Regla* translates as "rule," and I know many Christians who turn to our Lady of the Rule as a way of turning to Yemaya herself. And, despite what you may have heard from other sources, there is nothing wrong with this.

About this Book

I have been a devoted child of Yemaya for thirty-five years. My life, my work, and my art have been dedicated to her. I have known her blessings, and I have suffered through her lessons. Like the sea, she provides and punishes. She gives life and takes it back. Her mercy and compassion know no bounds, but neither does her anger. Like a good son, I try my best never to disappoint or anger her. In fact, incurring her wrath is something I wouldn't wish on my very worst enemy. I know many people who have learned this lesson the hard way.

After the loss of my own mother in late 2016, Yemaya's role as my spiritual Mother became even more important and clear to me. In fact, it was only through my faith in her and my circle of family and friends that I survived. As I began to spiral into a deep depression, it was Yemaya Olokun who sent me back up to the surface from the darkest depths of despair, and brought me back into focus. This reconfirmed and cemented my devotion to her, to my faith, and to myself.

It has taken me years to come to my desk and write this book celebrating my beloved *Omio* (Mother). I didn't want to do it; for me, it represented a daunting Herculean task, and I simply refused many requests from my editor. I just didn't want to write a book on Voodoo, or Candomblé, or Ifa, or any religion. To me, religion is an extremely precious, private, and personal thing. My religious beliefs are mine and mine alone. Frankly, they are nobody's business, unless I decide to make them so.

Considering that I am often in the public eye, I've always been a very private person. So I put off writing this book for five years. I'm not really a nonfiction writer; I'm a poet. I speak in the language of the imagination; I craft stories to be related aloud; I am a spoken-word performer and a novelist. Truth be told, I was afraid of letting the world down. I didn't want to embarrass myself and the people who believed in me—the ones who kept pushing me to just sit the hell down and write. I heard this question over and over in messages, conversations, and emails: "How much different is it really from the classes and discussions you teach and host?" And then it hit me. I wouldn't write about religion at all. Instead, I would write about the life-long center of my faith—Yemaya. I've always loved telling her stories and teaching people about her, so why not?

So finally I began to write, to draw a few illustrations, and to take the handful of photos you find here. While the task still felt Herculean and impossible, I resigned myself to it. I hope I have done my job well. I hope this book conveys something of myself and my love for Yemaya.

As I wrote, the global pandemic of covid-19 was making its horrible presence known, spreading like a dark fog across the world, forcing us all into isolation, leaving us to find alternate ways to make enough money to feed our families. My shop closed for three months, during which time I began to make and sell face masks, sewing ten to twelve hours a day, every day, seven days a week to get my bills and rent paid. I received no help from the government despite the promises that my small business would be saved. I just put my faith in Yemaya, knowing that she would not let me or my family go hungry or go without the necessities of life and health. And as usual, she guided me to the abundance I needed. This evil virus and the deep-seated rifts in our society have divided our country and turned neighbor against neighbor, unleashing a level of discord and violence that is unprecedented.

There may never have been a time in the history of the world when the healing, cleansing waters of Yemaya are more desperately needed than they are today, and will be tomorrow. Every day, I turn to my shrine and beg the Mother of All Life to take control of her unruly children and keep them from harming other members of her enormous family. I implore her to sweep her healing waves across the planet in order to soothe the frightened and the angry, and open the eyes of those who cannot see the truth of the state we are in. I ask her to help those who are in despair and to heal the sick. That is who and what Yemaya is to me. She is the healing, the compassion, and the miracles we need. She is my faith—a faith I express in this prayer:

Radiant Thrice-Crowned Queen of Sea, Earth, and Moon,
For whom nothing is beyond your power,
Bringer of compassion and miracles,
Peace and harmony,
I humbly beg of you, wrap this world in your blue mantle
    of protection.
Let not evil or sickness or violence or anger invade our
    lives.
Keep the destructive power of this despicable disease away
    from your children;
Wipe it from this world, this universe, this reality.
Restore our communities, that our children may play to-
    gether once more,
That we may return fully to our jobs and responsibilities.
Keep us fed and clean.
Keep poverty away.
Great Mother, as I cling to the hem of your seven skirts for
    your blessings and protection,
Remember me in your prayers, as you remember all of your
    children on earth.
Oh glowing Star of the Sea,
I sing your praises;
I dance your holy rhythms.
Maferefun Yemaya.
Ashé Yemaya, Ashé
Yemaya be praised.

May she hear my prayer and grant my wish that the world be healed.

PART I

Yemaya—Mother of All Life

Yemaya Ibu Mayelewo

CHAPTER 1

The Power of the Goddess

When Olodumare gathered the gasses and minerals from the dust of the universe, they were already pregnant with the life force of Yembo, the primordial Mother. When she came into physical form, she brought fertility and potential birth into the world, becoming the Mother of All Life, whose dominion was the earth and the sea. She was constantly pregnant and bringing forth life, the waters of her womb becoming the seas and rivers. She gave birth to the first orishas and later, as Yemaya, to the first humans. In her mythos, all of her many aspects, often referred to as her "sisters," dwell with her within her living waters and are considered to be the royal spiritual family of the sea.

Yemaya's power over the primordial forces of nature derives from *Ashé*, a Yoruban word that means "life force." But Ashé is much more than that. Ashé is the pure, undiluted, glorious, glowing power found within every natural element, object, and place. It is the power within us on which we draw to manifest our desires and bring about change in the material world. It is the power that flows through the spirits and our ancestors. The force of creation, magic, and will. It is a term that can be used as a blessing in greetings and partings, and as a petition that all good things may be granted.

There is Ashé in the stones we fashion into dwellings, in the water we drink, in the fire that warms us, in the air we breathe, in the cities we inhabit and the countryside we enjoy. It is present in the plants we cultivate, the food we eat, and the animals all around us. It reaches out to us in the words of power spoken by our healers and religious leaders. It is our hope, our fate, our destiny. Quite simply, Ashé is everything and everyone, expressed as an anthropomorphized manifestation of the natural forces of the universe—wind, fire, water, earth, birth, death, healing, attraction, storms, tidal waves, and earthquakes.

Yemaya's original name, *Ye omo eja*, means the Mother of Fishes, because she has as many children as there are fish in her vast domain. She is now known by many other names, including Mother of All Life, Goddess of the Sea, Queen of the Sea, Mother of Compassion, Ocean Mother, primordial Mother, Queen of Magic, and many more. I even call her Big Mama. These names are interchangeable in most traditions, although not all traditions recognize or use them all.

Because of Yembo's associations with fertility and potential birth, it is said that Yemaya is greedy for sons, and often claims those born to other orishas as her own—a habit the other orishas do not seem to mind. Those she did not bear—like Shango, god of thunder, lightning, and fire, and the children of other spirits—she fostered. Oshun, goddess of love and attraction, in particular is well-known for releasing her children into the care of the great oceanic Mother. More concerned with having fun and being free than she is with motherhood, Oshun seems to feel that Yemaya can do a better job of raising her offspring than she can.

Yemaya's desire for sons and daughters is driven by a spiritual goal—to grow her priesthood and community of practitioners and

Lemanja

ensure its continuing presence and power throughout the world and into the future. She is often depicted in stories as sacrificing herself for the good of her children and her kingdom. Her progeny secure her place in the universe and make her *Omi Leto*, the axis upon which all things turn. Without her blessings, nothing on the earth or in the sea could exist.

Finding Yemaya

I first encountered Yemaya when I was about eight years old. My family and I had gone to stay for a couple of days in a rented beach house. There was a jetty fairly close to the shore and, despite the warnings of my mother, I waded out to it at low tide and climbed up on the rocks. I did. Of course I did. My fascination with the ocean was already firmly established and there was no way I was going to give up the chance to sit on the rocks surrounded by the lapping waves. The sun was strong and bright; the flashes of light reflecting off the ripples in the water were hypnotic. The rhythm of the waves beating against the jetty was like the beating of a great heart, so unbelievably soothing that I fell asleep on the cool rocks.

As I slept, the tide came in and began to cover the narrow jetty. Although the rock I had dozed off on was at the jetty's highest point, it was also the farthest from the shore. I panicked. Although I loved the water, I was not yet a good swimmer and the darkness of the waters frightened me. I began to cry.

That is when she came. I watched her glide across the waves in an almost Christ-like fashion. She was beautiful—beautiful in a way that human speech cannot explain or describe. She was tall and caramel-skinned. Her impossibly long ebony hair was unbound and streaming in the wind. She glittered in the sunlight. She wore a shift-like white dress that covered little more than the water could have. I looked up at her through tear-stung eyes and heard her words. Though her lips never parted, her voice was everywhere. She told me to stop crying, that I would be fine and was safe. She said she had come to help me and that, one day, we would meet again. Her smile evaporated all my eight-year-old tears and fears. I felt warm and loved and protected, and I drifted peacefully back to sleep.

Some time later, I awoke on the sandy shore to hear my mother calling for me to come in for dinner. To this day, I don't really know if I actually dreamed the whole incident. Did I never leave the sand? Did I really wade out to the rocks and fall asleep? Did I merely dream about the beautiful lady on the water? I choose to believe it was real.

Thus began my obsession with mermaids, water goddesses, the ocean, and everything within it. My collection of seashells, mermaid figurines, and books about sirens and mermaid lore grew, eventually becoming a dragon's horde so large that I had to give some of it away lest it completely engulf my home. But I replaced those gifted items over and over, so that my collection became like the tide—always renewing itself and never ending. This childhood experience began my life-long search for the radiant lady who had come to me in my hour of need.

It took a few years and a near-death experience—I would have to die and be resuscitated before I found her—but, eventually, I discovered Yemaya's identity and began to explore her traditions. When I did, the purpose of my life changed and I turned to her in devotion.

A few years after this seaside visitation, I was in a very bad accident. I was crushed beneath a stack of plywood while playing around a house that was under construction. As my friends ran to get help, I clawed my way out from under the landslide of wood, tearing my back and face to shreds on the way before passing out in a broken heap on the other side. I can remember waking up very briefly in my father's car with my mother holding a towel tight against my face. I heard someone singing (it was Stevie Nicks on the radio) and then—nothingness. No white light, no parade of ancestors or people I knew who had passed. Simply nonexistence. Kind of.

I still experienced some form of consciousness, but I had no individual form. I was connected to everything, everywhere, all at once. My spirit seemed to be floating in a sea of warm gray comfort. It was slow and gentle, and I even felt happy. I could sense and hear others all around me; we were all together. It was beautiful.

I don't know how long I floated in the psychic waters of the next world before Yemaya came to me. It seemed as if many years passed, but come she did. In her crystalline voice, the lady I had encountered on the water told me that I had to leave the warm comforting sea in which I was floating. I had to go back. She had work for me to do before I could go down the river to the "old folks at home." She told me that the person I had been before no longer existed. She said that I had been given a gift—a new name, a task to perform, and a difficult road to travel. I would know many losses and sorrows; I would face many trials and tribulations. But I would also help many people in her name. When I woke up in the hospital a few days later, nothing would ever be the same again.

My relationship with Yemaya has, over the last few decades, become more of a lifestyle than a religious faith. There is no part of my life, or even of my world, that is not directly affected by or influenced by this deep spiritual connection. I have kept lavish altars piled with flowers, candles, statues, and offerings, along with strings of pearls, seashells, and mermaids. Art prints and my own paintings depicting the goddess are spread throughout my home and shop, taking over all the space they can. Yemaya loves beautiful and lavish things. Big Mama has expensive tastes and, if it were up to her, she would take over the entire house and shop for herself. Although in lean times, I have been forced to keep simple, plain, humble altars, my connection to the goddess and my faith in her have never faltered.

Embracing Yemaya

When you embrace Yemaya, she comes into your life like a great wave, encompassing and filling your existence with love and magic. A few years ago, as I was out shopping with my husband, Malcolm, I came across a beautiful tureen that was shaped like an exceptionally large nautilus shell, with a gilded base and lid. It was (and still is) breathtaking. As I was admiring the costly work of art, I heard the ocean waves clear as a bell and was struck by the scent of salt water. Clearly, Yemaya wanted this tureen to keep her tools in, rather than the plain white ceramic one that I used at the time. Unfortunately, I could not afford this luxury, so I bargained with the goddess, promising that, if she helped provide the finances to pay all the bills and rents for that month, I would return and gladly purchase the tureen for her if it was still there.

The next day, I was deluged with clients who wanted readings and spell work and, by the end of the day I had literally twice what I needed to justify purchasing the tureen. Needless to say, Big Mama still has that gilded shell tureen front and center on her altar in my home. That same year, she also demanded a huge wrought-iron mermaid holding a scallop-shell candle holder. She still has this as well. Yemaya has a habit of getting her way—and whatever she wants, when she wants it.

I have lived by the water where I hear Yemaya's voice most clearly, and I have lived in cities where I have had to build a substitute ocean to facilitate clearer communication (see chapter 11). But in every place I have ever lived, the goddess has unmistakably made her presence felt, and that presence is reflected in my surroundings.

When you turn to Yemaya, nothing in your life remains unchanged. You begin to feel and see her influence and power in everything you do. And as your relationship with her grows, this becomes more and more evident. I am not surprised that many Neo-pagans and witches are becoming more and more attracted to her. She represents the primordial beginnings of life on this planet. She is the well-spring of creation and magic. She is the deep unknown, the hidden knowledge that we, as spiritual beings, search for our whole lives. She can seem mysterious and exotic to some; she can feel like family and home to others. She embodies all human emotion. She knows our most secret dreams and desires and can lead us to them as long as we surrender to her influence.

In fact, followers call Yemaya the spirit of surrender. But this doesn't mean that she wants us to give up. Rather, she wants us to give in to the ebb and flow, the tides, of life. She tells us not to struggle against them. Swimming against the tide does no good. We struggle to stay in one place until we are too weary to continue. But if we just surrender to the flow, we are swept out into the endless sea of potential and opportunity, where we become boundless.

Mother of Compassion and Renewal

Yemaya is often portrayed as the Mother of Compassion. In this role, she seeks to heal and comfort the sorrows of her children, who often gather at the shore to tell her of their dreams, their woes, their losses, and their pain. There is no illness, depression, or despair that she cannot heal, no corruption or negativity she cannot wash clean. When called on with an honest open heart, she can take all our afflictions to the bottom of the sea and drown them, releasing us from pain and suffering. But when her children petition her for help, they are always extremely careful not to enter the water when they do so, because so great is her love and her desire to comfort her sons and daughters that she may sometimes pull them into the depths and back to her womb.

Most of the prayers we recite to the Ocean Mother are concerned with keeping us protected from evil, poverty, sickness, death, and sorrow. She is always there in our time of need, manifesting in the physical world in many ways—sometimes as a scent of watermelon or seawater where there is none. Sometimes she appears in the form of a beautiful dark-skinned woman in blue-and-white skirts. She has been known to show herself in the guise of a fierce pirate queen and sometimes as mermaids that appear to you randomly on your travels. Like all the orishas, she walks the earth in various forms, however she sees fit, seeking to help us on our journey through this chaotic and often dangerous world.

Yemaya is the spiritual mother to whom we cry when the harshness of the world becomes unbearable. We cling to her skirts and weep into the lace of her hems as she comforts us and rocks us to the rhythm of the tides, until we become calm and regain our composure and the strength to carry on. She gives us advice through signs and oracles, speaking through cowrie shells (see chapter 11) and through the priests and priestesses she possesses in ceremonies. She whispers to us in dreams and visions, watching over us in the silvery light of her lunar aspect. She is the mother who turns no one away.

Yemaya's power is also felt in the collective consciousness, as we are all created from her waters and carry them within. We are thus all linked in a never-ending global sea of inspiration and psychic connectedness, pulled and pushed by the lunar tides and the waters of the unconscious. Her tides rock us; her crashing waves energize us; the light reflecting on the surface of her oceans comforts us; the salt air of her kingdom fills us with memories. Big Mama is always around us, always holding us, always protecting us.

Many Neopagans, witches, and others outside the traditions of Yemaya's African homelands tend to isolate this power of compassion and healing, as if this is all she can be. But the truth is that the Ocean Mother is as vast and deep and changeable as her domains. People tend to look at her as Mother Nature or as the Earth Mother, with all that comes with this portrayal—fertility and life-giving energies all bundled up and tossed into the sea. But Yemaya constantly swells and expands. She evolves. The Yemaya who arrived in Cuba, the birthplace of Santeria, is a far cry from her original form as the goddess of the Ogun River in Nigeria. The Iemanja who settled in Brazil is different from both her Cuban incarnation and her Haitian aspects. The Yemaya of English-speaking countries is farther still from her African roots.

Wherever Yemaya travels, she acquires attributes, dominions, folklore, and practices that the original river spirit would be at a loss to recognize as her own. In fact, we cannot confine Yemaya to any one aspect or power or tradition any more than we can keep the entire ocean in a fishbowl. She is far too expansive. Unfortunately, many act as if they can. Some even go as far as to claim ownership of the goddess—as if any mortal can own a force of nature. Some seek to keep others from worshipping her.

There are some who think that, to know Yemaya, you must be African; others say only Hispanics have a right to worship her. Some say only Brazilians can serve her properly. I find this selfish, self-important, and egotistical. All witches who worship Hecate are not Greek, just as all who worship Isis are not Egyptian. Not all devotees of Rhiannon are Welsh. Does this lessen the authenticity of their love and devotion? No, it certainly does not. And as all life began in the waters of Yemaya's kingdom, all the peoples of earth have an innate connection to her. The Mother of All Life is the mother of all races by the very definition and purpose of her role in the universe. Divine mothers do not turn away their children because their skin is too light or too dark. The Ocean Mother does not discriminate. Only humans do that.

There is a very popular yoga mantra that goes like this: *Yemaya Assessu, Assessu Yemaya, Yemaya Olodo, Olodo Yemaya.* This translates roughly to: "Yemaya is the Gush of the Spring. The Gush of the Spring is Yemaya." This chant speaks of the eternal evaporation and replenishing of the waters of Yemaya's kingdom. In it, she becomes, not only the giver of life, but also of rebirth. And, in becoming so, she also becomes the owner of reincarnation.

Charlie and the Light

I end this chapter with a story about Charlie, one of my initiates. It is a tale of self-worth and renewal, and the compassion of Yemaya in her Mother aspect.

One night during the year of his initiation, Charlie went down to the ocean to pray to Yemaya, a practice with which he was well acquainted and which he often performed. But this night proved to be different from the hundreds of other nights he had done the same ritual. This night seemed dimmer. As he looked out at the vastness of the ocean, overwhelmed by his emotions and his self-doubt, he felt small and insignificant. He felt unworthy and wondered why he was even there. These thoughts and feelings swirled like a chilly wind all around him.

As Charlie looked out into the incoming waves, he noticed a tiny light flashing on the water. It came closer and closer, until he could see that it was, in reality, a lightning bug that had flown too close to the waves and had been pulled into the water. Charlie, a child of Yemaya, scooped the tiny flashing creature from its impending doom and gently placed it on a tree stump. He sat there bewildered, until the lightning bug's wings were dry enough for it to fly away.

In a flash of understanding, Yemaya's mercy became crystal clear to Charlie. He became aware of his own worthiness of her love and admiration. If this tiny blinking speck of life, this little creature, was worthy of Yemaya's mercy and compassion, then how could he not be? His heart swelled with a renewal of sorts, as he realized the interconnectedness of this entire experience. Because, in the moment he saved the lightning bug, it was as if he had acted as its god, interceding on its behalf. He had held its tiny life in his gentle hands. And all of this had been orchestrated by the Ocean Mother, the Mother of Compassion.

CHAPTER 2

The Many Faces of Yemaya

Like the ocean from which she was born, Yemaya is infinitely variable and supremely powerful. Her personality has many facets, many aspects. She travels many *caminos* (roads) and appears with many different faces. Just as part of me is a poet, another is a painter, another a doll-maker, and yet another a psychic reader. Whenever I am completely submerged in any of these roles, I am a very different version of myself. Likewise, when Yemaya is fully submerged within different aspects of her personality, she literally becomes a new version of herself, with different likes and dislikes, different practices and taboos, different responsibilities in the universe, and different names to go with each version.

In African Traditional Religions, only a priest can tell you what aspect of Yemaya is focused on your life. But in your own personal spiritual practice, you can invoke whatever aspect of Yemaya you need most in your life—although I suggest sticking with the totality of Yemaya that encompasses all of these pathways. And that is the Yemaya portrayed and honored in this book.

Nonetheless, I believe it would be a disservice to both you and the goddess not to give you some basic information about the most well-known aspects of the Ocean Mother. As we have seen, all these aspects are said to exist simultaneously, yet individually, and are often referred to as her "sisters." So if Yemaya Olokun is the ocean, the many spirits who live within its living waters are her spiritual family. These aspects of Yemaya are not interchangeable, however. Each aspect is considered an individual and must be treated respectfully as such.

Depending on the tradition, the practice, or the part of the world you are in, these aspects may differ. Yemaya changes everywhere she goes, becoming whatever people most need her to be. Like water itself, the goddess is fluid and constantly transforms herself. And like the ocean, she is fathomless. The differences in traditions can and will bring up disagreements in the defining of Yemaya's avatars, but this is to be expected.

You'll find a more complete listing of these aspects and person-alities in the Appendix, but here are some of the best-known faces of the goddess.

Ibu Achaba

In her aspect as Ibu Achaba, the first female diviner, Yemaya stole the secrets of the cowrie shells from her then-husband Orunmila, the spirit of divination. Cowrie shells are used as a divination tool in Yorubaland in the same manner that runes, coins, or yarrow stalks are used in other divinatory systems. Yemaya used Orunmila's cowrie shells to support herself by reading for his clients when he was away on long journeys. This act of independence brought about the end of their marriage. Ibu Achaba prefers to wear the colors turquoise, green, and yellow, and only speaks to her children with her back to them. Her name means "anchor" and she is referred to as "she who comes from heaven."

Yemaya (hand painted and beaded canvas with more than ten thousand hand-sewn beads, sequins, and cowrie shells)

Ibu Agana

This avatar of Yemaya is married to the orisha Oko, the god of agriculture. This is a very angry aspect of the goddess, and her relationship with Oko had serious consequences for mankind. In this role, Yemaya's name is translated as "crazy" and this is at once the most and least attractive of her aspects. Ibu Agana's face is surpassingly beautiful but, like a calm sea, her visage hides potential destruction beneath the waves. Her body is marred by seven cysts on her belly. One of her legs is also smaller than the other. This causes her to limp and hinders her ability to dance, which brings both shame and anger into her heart. She resides at the very bottom of the sea and has ties to Oroina, the spirit of the magma of volcanoes, as well as to cosmic radiation and the heat of the sun.

Ibu Assessu

This aspect of Yemaya is found where the water is still and brackish, and where the frothy white foam of the sea touches the dry sand. She appears as the waves crash onto the shore, clothed in sky blue. She is also found where springs gush up from the earth. This forgetful aspect of Yemaya needs to be reminded to answer her children's prayers, which she does very slowly. We do not pray to her for things urgently needed, but rather for things that need a lot of time to grow. Ibu Assessu is the owner of ducks and geese. She spends her time counting the feathers on a duck, then beginning again when she loses count—endlessly, like the tides.

Ibu Elowo

Ibu Elowo is Yemaya in her aspect as the expansiveness of the sea. She is the owner of all the riches of the ocean and the keeper of all sunken treasures lost since the beginning of time. This aspect can easily be compared to a mermaid living in a treasure-filled grotto at the bottom of the sea where no one can hope to reach her wealth.

Ibu Mayelewo

Ibu Mayelewo is the favored daughter of Olodumare, the supreme creator god. She lives in the middle of the sea where the seven tides mingle. This aspect of Yemaya is very prideful and judgmental, preferring to look at people only from the corner of her eye. She is often seen wearing a mask, carrying a serpent, and holding a fan of coral. Once married to the orisha Oko, the god of agriculture, she now lives at the bottom of the sea with Olokun and acts as his messenger.

She gave the ocean waters their color. She is a superior business-woman, and her name means "one who loves money." She can be immensely helpful in matters of finance.

Ibu Okoto

This aspect of Yemaya is associated with pirates, and we find her wherever blood has been shed in the water. This fierce aspect is a very formidable warrior who is associated with the color navy blue. She is eager to go into battle. She fights with scimitars and daggers, and, unlike most manifestations of Yemaya, she prefers to wear pants when she rides to war. In this aspect, Yemaya abandons Ogun, the god of iron and progress who raped her in her first incarnation as Yembo, and returns to her own house, where she turns her focus to ensuring the good of her kingdom.

Ibu Okunté

This furious warrior aspect of Yemaya steps out of the sea each winter as snow and ice, but only in the Western hemisphere. Hence this aspect is not found in the goddess's original Nigerian homeland. Her temper is horrible, and she never forgets a slight or insult. We give her ice instead of salt water on her altar, and her children fare much better in the winter months.

Okunté is married to Ogun, the spirit of iron, and lives with him in the forest. She stays by the lakes and streams. She goes into battle with machetes, wearing a chain from which hang her husband's tools. She smokes cigars and prefers the colors cobalt blue and red. Okunté created the oceans and lives in the reefs, where she adorns herself with red coral and pearls. She stands just outside the gate of Olokun's kingdom and allows visitors in and out. She refuses ducks and hates dogs, having once beheaded one who bit the hem of her skirt. Her children do not keep dogs in their homes, unless they balance the energy with a snake. She often sends rats as messengers.

Yemaya Atarawa

Yemaya Atarawa is easily the wealthiest avatar of the goddess. She is the owner of all the riches of earth and sea. Though her home is in the depths, she guards the coastline where plants and grasses grow wild. She is called on in matters of finance and wealth. She is opulent, benevolent, and regal. She protects the coastline and the plants and animals that make their home there.

Yemaya Ibu

Very little is known about this aspect of the goddess. She lives with her sister Oshun in the rivers and goes on land only to meet with her lover, Agayu, who is the spirit of the volcano and the embodiment of all of nature. She offered Agayu her sister Oshun as a bride in order to free herself from their relationship. Her role in the universe is not clearly defined, and her path has been obscured.

Yemaya Ibualaro

In some traditions, Yemaya Ibualaro is the arbiter of life and death. What she gives, she can take back. A stern and imposing figure, she rises from the waves with the gift of life in one hand and death in the other to survey vessels or people lost at sea. She decides who will survive the waters and who will not. In this way, she is an equalizing force, although we don't really know how or why she makes these decisions.

Yemaya Ibuina

Yemaya Ibuina is the queen of tragedy and conflict. She is present during all trials and misfortunes (*osobogos*). This avatar of the goddess is known for her harsh attitude, her blunt demeanor, and her tendency to be forward. She is an arrogant debater who never sugarcoats anything she says, regardless of the arguments or even wars (which she loves) it may cause. In my house, we turn to her only when we, or the spirits, want the blunt unvarnished truth. She is not a kind or loving aspect and prefers war to love.

Yemaya Ogunosomi

This sister of Okunté lives on the surface of the water and has a fondness for mountains. As a warrior aspect of Yemaya, she accompanies Shango, god of thunder, lightning, and fire, and Ogun, god of war and iron, into battle carrying two machetes. Nonetheless, she is very beloved for her ability to heal the sick. She is often petitioned to turn the tides of illness and return health to the afflicted.

Yemaya Oro

Yemaya Oro is the singing mermaid. She lives with the dead of the sea—the drowned and the shipwrecked—and reigns over them. She is mysterious and stays hidden. In this form, she is most siren-like, but, instead of singing to lure the unwary into fatal danger, she sings to the dead to comfort them. She haunts sunken ships and wreckage lost in the darkest parts of the ocean, unseen by all but the dead.

Yembo/Yemmu

Yembo is the first incarnation of Yemaya and the true crown of the goddess. She is the mother of all orishas and cosmic Mother of All Life as we know it. Yembo gave birth to the stars, the moon, and the sun. After Olodumare, the supreme creator god, placed the souls in each of the orishas, she delivered them into physical bodies. She is considered to be *orisha funfun*, which means "white orisha." She displays ties to Oddua (the female aspect of Obatala, Father of the World) and is the serenity and calm of the seashore. She appears in dazzling white dresses with pale-blue accents. Never give her metal as an offering, as it reminds her of her rape by Ogun, the orisha of iron.

Other Family Members

There are other members of Yemaya's spiritual family who, unlike the orishas, are separate from the goddess herself and from her aspects. Ikoko, for instance, has dominion over all aquatic plants, while Olose rules over lagoons. Crocodiles are her servants and some traditions depict her as being married to Olokun. Olona, another family member, lives in Yemaya's lakes and protects them from harm and the pollution of mankind.

There are also some misunderstood relations in the spiritual court of sea spirits and some deities of sister traditions that we should mention here because you will undoubtably run across them or hear about them at some point.

La Sirène, the Haitian *lwa* (spirit) of the ocean, appears as a beautiful and bewitching mermaid. She rules over music, the arts, beauty, and magic. Like Yemaya, her sacred number is 7, representing the seven seas and seven stars. But, unlike Yemaya, her colors are pale green, white, and pink. She teaches sorcery to humankind by taking aspirants with her under the sea for seven years, not allowing them to return until their term is done. *La baleine*, the whale, is her shadow self. Although this is reminiscent of Olokun, however, these are not interchangeable names or spirits. Rather, they are more like cousins. La Sirène is married to Admiral Agwé, the king of the sea.

Mami Wata, another branch of Yemaya's spiritual family, is not one specific spirit, but rather a blanket term for all the African water-spirit families. In modern times, the title has been anthropomorphized as a single water goddess, which is a misinterpretation of the original term. Nonetheless, belief and faith in this incarnation brings with it its own validity.

Nana Buruku is a family member whose name means "Grandmother Wicked." In some traditions, she existed before all other things, even Olodumare, the supreme creator god. In others, she came into being following the rape of Yembo by Ogun. It is said that Yembo's rage at being so defiled was so great that she was split into two distinct entities—Yemaya, who became the oceans, and Nana Buruku, who ascended to the moon, where she watches over mankind in the silver moonbeams, hidden from sight. She prefers to be alone and unseen and is very secretive. She is a frighteningly powerful witch. Her temper is horrible and dangerous, and her punishments are doled out swiftly and without mercy. Yet her love is just as strong and unyielding. Because she has never forgiven Ogun, you should never use metal knives to cut your offerings to her or to Yemaya.

Just as in most very large families with contrasting views, there are a lot of similarities and just as many differences between these spirits and aspects. In fact, there is no single correct path to the goddess. Each tradition may claim that theirs is the only way or that they have the final word, and those outside these traditions may find this confusing and frustrating. But don't be discouraged. No one owns the "rights" to the Mother of Fishes. No one.

CHAPTER 3

Mother and Lover

The ocean is often referred to as the womb of all life. However, in Yemaya's tradition, it is much more. It is also the desire to create life. The crashing of the waves against the rocks echoes the rhythm of the sacred drums. They mirror the pounding of the heart, the pulsing of our blood, and the throbbing of our lust, which aches to find its release and replenishment again and again, as the rain replenishes the river and the river replenishes the sea. In a similar way, Yemaya, as the Ocean Mother, and Olokun, as primal lust, reflect this dual drive toward sexuality and procreation.

Olokun is the deepest aspect of the ocean—the deep dark, where no light penetrates. Only Olodumare, the supreme creator god, and Olokun know what lies at the bottom of the sea. Olokun—who may be female, or male, or both—is the place from which the whirlpool churns, the place where the tidal wave gathers its strength. This is the primal aggressive nature of desire. You can no more deny the passion and relentless strength of Olokun than you can hold back the sea itself.

And it is even more impossible to resist the force of Yemaya Olokun when their aspects merge. From this combination of male and female energies, an entire ocean of primal pleasure emerges and the infinite capacity for ecstasy is realized. This energy makes its presence known in the salty rivulets of sweat that drench our heated skin during sexual encounters and the pheromones that lure us with the scent of sex in which we drown.

That essence, that primordial desire, is why lovers stroll and make love on the beach, why poets write about the "sea of love" and "sailing to paradise." It's the romance of the Islands and the spray on your skin that caresses you like a lover. It's the way the water engulfs you and the never-ending longing call of sea birds. The ceaseless pull of the tides and the moon on the water within us. Our fertility itself comes from this sexual power.

But are Yemaya and Olokun two separate entities, or are they one and the same? In many traditions, Yemaya and Olokun are considered to be separate. In others, they are understood to share a symbiotic relationship, sometimes referred to as father and daughter, sometimes as husband and wife. Sometimes they are even protrayed as sisters, or represented as a two-headed hermaphroditic being.

Divine Lovers

In the role of divine lover, Yemaya seduces and beguiles like a siren— the hypnotic sway of her hips, the scent of the sea that clings to her hair, the salt crystals that shimmer diamond-like on her dark skin as she rises from the waves into the moonlight, capturing the hearts and dreams of sailors who long to be in her embrace forever and pine for the sea when stuck too long on dry land. As in classical tales of mermaids stealing the hearts (and virility) of men, she encompasses all desires, even those so deep within that we do not know or understand them. The fog rolling across the still waters is her sweet breath against the ear, the temptation and compulsion to dive in.

Yemaya has been married to several male orishas, including Obatala (Father of the World), Orula (god of prophecy and divination), Oko (god of agriculture), Inle (god of health and healing), Agayu (god of erupting volcanoes), and Babalu Ayé, who heals the land and supports the elderly. Before Oshun, the youngest orisha, walked the earth, it was Yemaya who fell prey to the lust-filled eyes of those who wished to possess her. But the ocean cannot be possessed and, true to her nature, the tides of Yemaya's heart turned and she grew bored with her husbands one by one and left them, returning to her ocean domain.

But Yemaya was never alone for long. At one point, she embarked on a somewhat incestuous relationship with her foster son, Shango. Their frequently flirtatious behavior is undeniable. In one famous story, Shango attempts to seduce Yemaya, having forgotten that she was essentially his mother. She responds by taking him into the ocean in a small boat and, becoming a tidal wave, threatening to drown him (see chapter 6). Shango fears only two things: the dead and Yemaya's waters.

In her aspect as lover, Yemaya is vain and proud. She expects to be showered with romance and seduced with exotic gifts of glowing sea pearls and platinum, corals, and glittering gems. She is offered sweet perfumes, abalone combs for her hair, and silver mirrors in which to admire her own beauty. There is power in her sexuality and strength—and she *knows* it. Moreover, she knows how to use that power and strength. She can be sweeter than molasses syrup (her favorite) or salty like her oceans. She can love you one moment and drown you the next—which is, of course, the very nature of her realm.

Olokun, however, hasn't been as lucky in love. He is chained beneath the sea so he won't flood the land, something he desires to do eternally as the result of a betrayal and a broken heart (see chapter 6). Olokun's heartbreak derives from his rejection by Oko, the god of agriculture. Olokun was in love with Oko but feared his love would be rejected due to his appearance—he was half man, half sea serpent. He went to Obatala, who was also once married to Yemaya, and asked for his council. Obatala told Olokun that he would grant him human form for one year and that, within that year, Oko would grow to love him so intensely that Olokun's true form wouldn't matter.

Olokun took this as a promise and went to court Oko. When Olokun found him and professed his love, Oko was so taken with him that he fell in love at first sight. They lived as lovers on the land for a year, until Oko discovered Olokun's true form as half man, half monster. He immediately rejected him, mocking his strange appearance and driving him in shame and sorrow back to the bottom of the ocean to brood and plot against those living on the surface.

The deeper meaning in Olokun's story, however, lies in his resulting hatred of liars and oath-breakers. He was promised by Obatala that Oko would not reject him—a promise that even the Father of the World could not keep. Obatala's broken promise and Oko's betrayal, along with the sheer number of two-faced people, liars, deceivers, and con artists in the surface world, disgusted Olokun to the point where, in his anger, he decided to wipe all life from the face of the earth and take back the land he had given to mankind to populate. And he nearly succeeded, flooding the world and battering it with tidal waves. Obatala finally put an end to this and chained Olokun to the bottom of the sea with a magical silver chain. There, when enraged, Olokun swims in violent circles, churning the water into whirlpools and waterspouts, and dragging human sailors to their death.

Very little is known about Olokun in the Western hemisphere outside of strict tradition. He is often improperly syncretized or compared to Poseidon, a deity with whom he has little in common beyond their associations with the sea. Many Neopagans and witches incorrectly use statues of one to represent the other on their altars, a practice that can only lead to disaster, as it courts the fierce anger of the deepest depths.

Sexual Ambiguity

And this brings us to the ambiguity—or rather the fluidity—of sexuality and gender in stories about Yemaya and Olokun. While most of Yemaya's aspects are decidedly female, Olokun is usually seen as either very masculine or androgynous, whichever he chooses to be. In our new world of non-binary gender roles and heteroflexibility, the relationship between Yemaya and Olokun becomes a beacon for these marginalized members of the community. This pair is like them; they feel like them; they love like them. They represent a source of divine love that understands and welcomes them without judgment or conditions or condemnation. In fact, orishas who inhabit multiple realms or who are shapeshifters—like Eshu, Olodumare, Logunede, Inle, Oya, and Ochumare—are often thought of as belonging to all genders (see below).

Because of this afinity, both Yemaya and Olokun have a special place of honor among their LGBTQ devotees, who find a welcoming home within this aspect of Yemaya. Many members of this community wish to have children; some adopt to fulfill that need. Some engage surrogates to carry and bear a child, while others arrange for one partner to play that role.

However, not all love-making is intended to result in children. Sex and pleasure for pleasure's sake is just as valid and driving and sacred. As author and witch Doreen Valiente wrote in her influential poem "The Charge of the Goddess": "For the Goddess hath said 'Behold all acts of love and pleasure are my worship.'" Here "all" means all acts of love and pleasure, not just procreative acts or heteronormative behavior. Does this mean that spending a Sunday afternoon in a bathhouse is akin to prayer or going to church? The answer to that is simple: Yes, at least for some.

As times change and we continue to develop and evolve, so does our sexuality—and so do our sexual identities and our preferences, kinks, and fetishes. Relationship roles change, as do relationships themselves. Polyamorous, open, and triad relationships are far more commonplace now, both within and outside of the Pagan community. Society has never been more exposed to these ideas than it is now. And while that same society has never been that great at accepting what it does not understand, it seems to be coming around to the realization that sex and love and pleasure are good things— that they don't need to be hidden away in dark corners and closets.

The surge of Yemaya's tides breaks down walls and barriers, and frees us—whether we are gay, straight, bi, trans, or asexual—to be who we are, who we are meant to be. There are always conflicting ideas about sexuality in African Traditional Religions, as well as in Neopaganism. Sadly, that will most likely always be the case. But people of all orientations and identities can look into the waters of Yemaya's mirror and see themselves reflected back.

In fact, Yemaya has become the matron saint of gay men and trans women. Two famous stories are related to this. In one, Yemaya is forced to disguise herself as a man for a time on an island inhabited exclusively by *adodi*—men with homoerotic attraction and behaviors. There, she falls in love with another man. In another story, a gaggle (because what is more fabulous than a gaggle!) of drag queens protects her from her homophobic husband's wrath and his fear and hatred of them. Suspecting her of homosexual tendencies, he immediately abandons his pursuit of her and leaves their marriage.

Historically, the level of acceptance of homosexuality by the orishas varies, as does its acceptance in the orisha traditions. If you ask where the gay priests are in Santeria, which has often been referred to as "the gay religion," the answer will often be *everywhere*, as Santeria is widely considered to be the most accepting of its LGBTQ members. Because of this acceptance, the visibility of these devotees is not compromised, something that is not true in Palo, where gays cannot be initiated by priests of the religion—allegedly, at least. I personally know gay initiates. Candomblé is another tradition with a large queer following.

Some spirits who are widely considered allies of the LGBTQ community include:

- Eshu, the trickster: Although this spirit is often graphically depicted with enormous male genitalia, Eshu also contains multiple powerful and prominent female manifestations. His sexuality is thought to be extremely fluid.

- Inle, hunter/fisher/healer: This spirit dwells where river and sea meet, merge, and mix, inhabiting the two realms simultaneously. He is also considered to be the doctor or physician for the other orishas. Depicted as extremely attractive, Inle dresses in fine clothes adorned with copious amounts of cowrie shells and gold beads. He has feminine features and long braids, and was once married to Yemaya, who cut out his tongue so he could not reveal her secrets. He became the lover of Abbata, whom Yemaya had rendered deaf so he could not hear anyone ask him about her secrets. Their connection was so strong that the deaf Abbata and the mute Inle were eventually able to communicate psychically.

- Logunede, son of Oshun (goddess of love and attraction) and Ochossi (god of archery and hunting): This spirit spends half the year dressed as a woman and half dressed as a man. He has become popular as the patron of transgendered and bisexual people, as well as of drag queens.

- Obatala, Father of the World: This spirit is king of the orishas and manifests as either male or female, as he/she chooses.

- Odulamare, supreme creator god: This god/goddess is not venerated or worshipped directly. Completely genderless, he/she is part of everything, and everything is part of him/her.

- Olokun, ruler of the deepest parts of the ocean: Olokun had a homosexual relationship with the orisha Oko, the god of agriculture. He is thought to be very gender fluid and is often pictured in contrasting images as very masculine or androgynous.

- Ochumare, the rainbow serpent: This spirit is the patron of artists, gay men, Lesbian women, and transgendered people. He is the movement of energy and light, as well as the owner of seasonal changes and cycles. He is symbolized by the rainbow, now a major LGBTQ symbol that is also regarded as Yemaya's crown. Seen as half human and half serpent, he is also the embodiment of transformative energy.

- Orula, god of prophecy: Orula, or Orunmila, left Yemaya to have a homosexual relationship with Ogun, god of war and iron. In many traditions, however, Orula is said to be very homophobic and Yemaya is given as the one who left.

- Oshun, goddess of happiness, love, sexuality, and attraction: Though decidedly female in manifestation, this spirit often chooses to ride (possess) male priests and accepts all demonstrations of love and sexuality. She has a strong homosexual following.

- Oya, goddess of wind: Oya has dominion over the air, the marketplace, and the cemetery. She rules over storms and feminine strength. Depicted as a fierce Amazon-like warrior, she accompanies Shango into battle wearing pants and a false beard. Oya has become a patron of strong Lesbian women.

- Pomba Gira, a spiritual collective: These spirits—who may be understood as one or many, or an entire category of spirits—have aspects that reign over sexual deviance, prostitution, burlesque performers, and outcasts. The Pomba Giras are mainly concerned with sex, death, and magic. They are matrons of women and gay men.

- Shango, god of thunder and lightning: Shango rules over male beauty, sexuality, and virility. He is so vain that he wears the same beaded headdresses as the female orishas, whose beauty he is said to rival. Although he has a reputation as a great womanizer, he is syncretized with Santa Barbara, the young virginal female saint. There are, however, conflicting stories of his acceptance of homosexuality, which I have found to generally reflect the prejudice of the person telling the story. It has been said that Shango and Eleggua shared such an afinity as to be of one heart.

Spiritual Home

There are other orishas, of course, who condemn or are ambivalent to the LGBTQ community, although in the *Regla de Ocha* (another name for Santeria), this seems to be the exception rather than the rule. As a gay man involved in African Traditional Religions, I have encountered some prejudices along the way. I've had readings from Santeros who said I wouldn't live past the age of thirty if I continued to sleep with men. Well, as I write, I'm fifty-one and still sleeping with men. I've had a few experiences in which I haven't been taken seriously by my peers, or have been left out of certain gatherings. But on the whole, I have found more acceptance than rejection—which I think speaks volumes about the place of LGBTQ people in these traditions. I've never really been in the closet and my views on sex have always been very fluid, something that worried me from time to time on my journey. But the worst of my fears never manifested.

Many gay men are drawn to Yemaya. For some, she is a substitute for the mother who rejected them. For others, it's her dual nature that appeals. As the siren, she represents a being who straddles the realms of earth and sea yet does not belong entirely to either. As Yemaya Olokun, the male and female aspects of the goddess are united in harmony and balance, and the lines dividing these energies become blurred and faded, if they exist at all. Most gay men can identify with this.

It is true that the gay male culture can be hyper-masculine; but it is also true that it can be intensely feminine. I think this is evident in the soaring popularity of the art of drag. I know more than one drag queen who embodies the spirit of Yemaya, and some who have even performed in her image (tastefully). And every drag queen has dressed as a mermaid at least once. I can't even guess the number of super-masculine muscle-gays who throw on a harness and fishtail and become the image of Olokun (even if they don't realize it), and how many hirsute gay men belonging to the Bear community strap on a clamshell bra, red wig, and mermaid tail and go full-on Ariel, belting out the lyrics to "Part of Your World."

Yemaya's appeal to the gay community is undeniable. She is beautiful, loving, and powerful. She is a strong, independent woman who rose to power through love, compassion, and suffering—a role we can relate to and in which we can see ourselves. Yemaya knows her place in the universe and celebrates it. She wears the rainbow, the ancient symbol of hope and the most recognized symbol of the LGBTQ community, as her crown. Yemaya's children—her devotees—are frequently practitioners of the performing arts, psychic readers, chefs, and artists. Members of the gay community have long had an incredibly strong and visual presence in these professions. The adoration of Yemaya in our community is palpable, and her influence on and inspiration for us is undeniable. For many of us, she is our spiritual home.

CHAPTER 4

Magician and Healer

Almost all aspects of Yemaya possess a mastery of witchcraft. She is wise and powerful, and her knowledge of spells is as vast and encompassing as the ocean itself. The constant churning of the sea empowers her and enables her to perform her magic twenty-four hours a day, every day. Her magic works with the tide, ebbing and flowing. Its effects can be subtle and gentle, or they can come crashing over you, flooding you with manifestation.

Yemaya reigns over all magic, and is often called on for help with psychic work, moon magic, fertility spells, healing, finances, and the making of potions. She rules over lucid and prophetic dreams, as the connection between the conscious and subconscious mind. But Yemaya always answers our calls in her own time. She strikes with unrivaled strength when she decides to and, because of this, shouldn't be called on for fast magic or things needed quickly, as she will likely not pay attention to any kind of human schedule. That is the purvue of other spirits, the ancestors, and our own personal magic.

Witches and other Neopagan practitioners who seek to incorporate Yemaya into their practices must focus on building a relationship with the goddess through offerings and daily prayer, rather than calling on her only in times of need, want, or despair. Veneration of Yemaya is not a matter of "dial-a-deity." It entails a lifestyle of service and servitude, a spiritual contract that must be entered into with a loving, trusting, true heart. When that is done, Yemaya returns our trust, love, and care in full measure. But always remember that any promise made to the Mother of All Life must be as binding as a notarized contract, for she will just as easily take back the gifts and abilities she bestows as a punishment for those she perceives as having broken their oaths to her.

As the Queen of Witches, Yemaya, in her travels, has influenced the magical works of other cultures in her guise as the Stella Maris. In Egypt, where she traded fins for feathers, she became Isis, the goddess of magic and life who is also a fierce warrior. This harks back to her watery beginnings, but, as Isis, the River Nile is her domain.

Water Magic

The phrase "sea witch" to me is such a sumptous title. It conjures up extremely specific images in the mind's eye of many—dark undersea caves, an eerily glowing cauldron, bottles of strange substances floating about, and an ancient hag cackling as her hair writhes in the current. Sometimes she is a beautiful sorceress haunting tidal pools waiting for her next human victim to fall prey to her dark charms.

There have been tales of sea hags in every nautical culture. They have even been popularized in modern movies, literature, and cartoons. But very rarely do we ever see these characters depicted in their true form—as the radiant Queen of the Sea, the Ocean Mother, and the Mother of All Life. In fact, the sea hag's magic is mainly protective in nature and her name is often invoked by sailors seeking safe passage and fishermen seeking full nets so they can feed their children. She blesses newlyweds with fertility and virility. Women who have difficulty conceiving often travel to the sea and lie in the shallows, allowing the waves to cover their wombs in the hope that the goddess will have mercy on them and allow them to bear children.

Water is a metaphysical portal through the veil between worlds. It carries power and acts as an exceptionally strong spiritual, psychic, and magical conduit. In many Christian traditions, baptisms are performed by pouring water over the heads of the faithful or by submerging them completely under water and reciting prayers over them. It is believed that, in that moment, the soul passes through the veil and is reborn fresh, clean, and renewed, ready to begin a new life. In New Orleans, Voodoo baptisms performed on St. John's Eve center around water as well.

Water also conducts electricity better than any other natural element and supports all of the four sacred elements. Without water, there is no fertile earth, and no fertile earth means no plants or trees. No plants or trees means no replenishment of breathable air and no source of fire to warm and comfort us. In fact, if we consider carefully, we find that water is the base of alchemy—the first ingredient or component in spell work, potion-making, magical baths, and cleansings, as well as the base element in chemistry and scientific experimentation.

Just as Yemaya is the bridge between the liquid and the solid, consciousness and the unconscious, she is also the bridge between the physical and the metaphysical. To quote my godson: "Witches are the scientists of the metaphysical." In fact, Yemaya's elemental power reigns over both worlds. This is seen even further in her connection to the tarot through her relationship to the High Priestess card.

The most popular version of the High Priestess tarot card is that from the Rider-Waite-Smith deck, created by artist Pamela Colman Smith. It depicts a blue-robed, veiled, and crowned queen who sits between two pillars, keeping them in balance. These pillars stand in front of the spiritual veil through which we can only pass with her leave. Beneath her foot is a crescent moon, one of Yemaya's symbols. The equilateral cross she wears can be interpreted as her influence over all four natural elements, not just her own. In her hands is a scroll of hidden wisdom that, in my opinion, represents esoteric knowledge, mystical learning, psychic workings, and magic—all of which are reigned over by Yemaya Olokun.

Beneath the waves—where no light passes, where strange glowing, blind-eyed fish hunt aimlessly, where people can never reach—dwells Olokun, bound by a heavy silver chain that prevents him from rising to the surface to destroy the world. As a great serpent-tailed siren, he is the deepest and most unknowable depths, not only of the ocean, but of the mind and heart as well. He is the absolute center of the subconscious, representing what is hidden and unknowable.

At the same time, Olokun is our deepest sorrows and most obfuscated passions. He is the desire and drive for vengeance against those who wrong us. He is the great flood, always seeking to take back the land that was stolen from him at the dawn of man. He is the broken heart that does not heal, but rather broods and waits for a chance to retaliate against the cause of his pain.

In my own times of darkest sorrow and most insurmountable heartbreak, I have turned to the great sea serpent—sometimes for solace, sometimes for healing, and, yes, frankly, sometimes for revenge. And no matter my reason for calling on him, he has always answered—although not always in the ways I would have liked or expected. Olokun is the keeper of knowledge forever lost to mankind and to time. This is why we say that only God and Olokun know what is to be found at the bottom of the sea. Seek him out for deeper understanding and to reveal hidden secrets. Although he is forever broken-hearted, he does not want you to suffer his sorrow and can be called on to take your burdens to the bottom of the sea and hold them there in his treasure-filled grottos and caves.

Healing Magic

Yemaya's power to heal is often displayed in dramatic ways. The very first time I sought Olokun's assistance, I was reeling in the aftermath of a seriously abusive relationship. I had been scarred emotionally, mentally, and physically. I had been abused and broken by someone who claimed to love me and whom I adored. My heart was ground into dust. I was continually afraid. I shunned all physical contact, as well as all social interaction. I could not trust. I didn't want to.

I lived in solitude, in an ocean of tears, pain, fear, and regret. All was darkness and despair. I became so overpowered by depression that I considered ending my time on this earth once and for all. Days melted into weeks and weeks into months. As the one-year mark arrived, I was no better. I completely neglected my health—emotional, physical, and spiritual. I phoned in my spiritual practices, going through the habitual actions without feeling or conviction. But there was no faith, no love, no belief in them anymore. Honestly, I just didn't care.

One night, I dreamed I was walking along the seashore, when the most breathtaking man I had ever seen swam up to me. He was dark-skinned and powerfully built, and had a long fish tail that resembled that of a dragon or serpent. He said: "Come to the shore, where the waves crash. Find the vessel and you will know what to do. I will take your pain to the bottom of the sea and drown it there."

I woke up instantly, got dressed in white clothing, and hurried to the beach, not really knowing what I was doing there or what I was supposed to look for. And then it appeared. As the gentle waves lapped at the shore, a beautiful chambered shell rolled up on the sand. As I picked it up, I began to cry—well, I full-on ugly-face sobbed, actually. I put the shell to my face and let my tears fall into it as I relived all the betrayal, hurt, and pain of my failed relationship, remembering the broken ribs and black eyes, until the shell overflowed with the salty effluence of my despair. I wrapped the shell in my white head scarf and threw it as far as I could into the ocean. Then I scattered silver coins all over the sand where I stood and made my way home.

I did not dream that night. Instead, I slept more deeply than I had in a year. In the morning, I got out of bed and sat in front of my mirror. I didn't look as sad and tired as I had only a few short hours before. There was something in my eyes that had been gone for so long. I felt happy. I knew then that the visitor in my dream was Olokun and that perhaps it had not been a dream at all, but a vision. Whatever the case, I knew he had taken my tears and pain to the endless depths of his realm and would keep them there forever.

Within days, I became more devoted to my spiritual duties and, within a month, I had opened myself up to a new love and begun a much healthier relationship. And although I was aware that I would one day feel pain again, I felt that I now had the strength to go through it and come out the other side alive and well.

Practicing magic with Yemaya has given me the most beautiful experiences of my life. Ministering to her children has filled the life that once I was so willing to end with purpose and meaning. I sing the praises of the Ocean Mother with every breath I take.

Stories of Yemaya's healing magic abound. I once had a student who had a serious medical issue that could have ended in tragedy. He was training to become a devotee of Yemaya and was very devout in his practices and his faith. One day in the kitchen at his office, the coffee maker spewed scalding-hot water over his head. Badly burned, he was understandably shocked and confused as to why such a thing would happen to him. After all, he was a child of the waters. Shortly thereafter, he went to see his doctor to discuss the possibility of surgery to correct his previously existing condition. To his shock, the doctor told him that his condition had, quite literally and unbelievably, vanished. The Ocean Mother had burned it away. My student's faith in her was cemented and, from that day on, he has been a most devoted child, blessed and highly favored by Yemaya.

I also knew a woman who was one of the nicest, kindest, most loving and giving people that I have ever known. For reasons unknown to me (because honestly, I never asked), her granddaughters, with whom she had been very close and whom she adored beyond the telling of it, had maliciously turned their backs on her with absolutely no explanation. I had been reading cards for this woman for years and, when she came to me distraught and in tears, I offered her my advice.

I instructed her to go to a local beach just before high tide and bring a watermelon and white roses. She was to sit on the sand and cry out to Yemaya, a spirit who was unfamiliar to her and of whom she was unaware at the time. I told her to empty her heart and spill her tears until they would no longer fall, then to roll the watermelon into the seawater and leave the roses at the waterline for the sea to take away. Finally, I told her to light a blue candle in Yemaya's name every day for seven days, suggesting that, if she did this, her grandchildren would return to her.

Warily, she took my advice and did as I told her to do. About two or three months later, her granddaughters had returned with apologies, tears, and explanations. After that, this woman was so grateful to Yemaya that she commissioned me to paint a portrait of the goddess for her. As far as I know, this still hangs in a place of honor in her home. I later cast spells of healing for her during her battle with cancer, which, by the grace of the goddess, she survived. Yemaya be praised.

I cannot even begin to count the many customers who stop in front of the huge shrine I keep to Yemaya in my shop and silently ask for her help and healing. They later return with small offerings of gratitude to place on the sparkling blue fabric that drapes the altar. I have recommended variations of these simple entreaties to hundreds of clients over the years, with varying rates of success. You can find some of them in more detail in chapter 11.

Oshun's Magical Journey

The power of water cannot be denied. It can be corrosive, reducing rock to sand over time. If there is the slightest crack or pinhole in a structure, water will find it and use it to its advantage. Water is always striving for balance, and seeks its own level no matter what it needs to do to get there. It, like Yemaya, is relentless in the pursuit of its goals. No matter how long it takes, water inevitably gets its way. Just like the Queen of the Sea.

I'll end this chapter with a story that demonstrates how Yemaya's magic, like the magic of all water, is transformative. In her hands, all things become fluid and malleable.

When the children of Yemaya and Oshun were being imprisoned and taken away on slave ships to be sold like cattle in the New World, this alarmed Oshun, so much that she ran to her sister, the Ocean Mother. When she arrived at Yemaya's palace, Oshun's eyes were swollen with tears. She sobbed as she begged her sister to intercede and help her look after her children in these strange new lands. "Please sister," she cried, "you who are the Mother of Compassion and Mistress of Miracles, the mighty Queen of Witches, must have a way to help me."

Yemaya thought about this for a moment and said: "I will give you a gift that will allow you to travel in the rain and waters so that you can follow your children."

Oshun seemed happier after that, but soon she began to worry. She looked at her dark skin and black hair and again turned to her sister. "Sister," she said, "you have traveled all over this world in the waves and rain, surely you must know. Do all the people there look like us? Do they all have our dark skin and hair?"

"No, little one," Yemaya replied. "There are many differences across the world. Some people are pink-skinned with golden hair and eyes as blue and green as my seas. Others are red-skinned and their black hair is long and straight and smooth as silk. Some are brown like us, in every shade."

"But what if the people won't accept me?" she asked. "I may not be able to stay with my children."

Yemaya could hear the great sadness in her sister's voice and thought for a moment. Then she took a sea sponge and dabbed it all over Oshun's face and body. As she did, her skin became a lighter shade, somewhere between brown, red, and pink. Oshun smiled as she admired her new honey complexion. Next, Yemaya picked up her own silver brush, which was decorated with mother of pearl and coral, and began to brush Oshun's hair. With each stroke of the brush, her hair became longer, straighter, and lighter, until it cascaded like an auburn waterfall tumbling in soft waves to her waist. Oshun's tresses now rivaled the length and beauty of Yemaya's own.

"Sister, you are truly the Queen of Magic," Oshun gushed.

"And now, little one, no matter how far you travel or where you settle, all people everywhere will see a little of themselves in you. You will be accepted in every country of the world that treasures love and beauty, and you will never have to be far from your children ever again."

With that Oshun traveled wrapped in the rain, following the slave ships that held her people. They led her to Cuba, where, thanks to Yemaya's great gift for magic, she settled and become the matron of that country.

CHAPTER 5

Warrior and Scourge

Yemaya has many warrior aspects. Each is a fearsome and almost Amazonian manifestation of the punishing sea. Some of these aspects go into battle alone; some accompany other warrior orishas like Shango and Ogun.

In her warrior aspects, Yemaya fights with flashing eyes and gnashing teeth, with machetes, axes, daggers, and scimitars. Wearing sea snakes around her shoulders and arms, she is the storm at sea, the violent waves, and the dragging, drowning undertow. She is the tidal wave that threatens to destroy the world and sweep all life back into her womb. These aspects of the goddess hold grudges. They neither forgive nor forget, and they deal with any slight or offense swiftly and harshly.

Water's ability to erode even the strongest stone and metal (other than lead) is symbolized in the tales of the warrior aspects of Yemaya. As a water goddess, Yemaya displays a relentless, never-ending, grinding determination to seek out the smallest crack in the armor of an enemy and focus on it until it is destroyed. Just like water, she always seeks her own level, no matter what the situation, and works nonstop until that level is achieved, breaking through both natural and man-made barriers and obstacles. All mountains eventually crumble into the sea; islands sink and their civilizations vanish (think of Atlantis). Virtually all cultures possess their own myth of a great flood caused by angry divinities who unleash the rain and the ocean's power and watch them consume everything in punishment for human hubris. Coincidence? Maybe, but I think not.

Yemaya can have important negative impacts on our physical health through water as well. Consuming too little water can affect your health and eventually kill you. But consuming too much water can cause a kind of drunkenness that can lead to serious health issues, overloading kidneys and rendering them unable to remove excess fluid from the body. When excess water builds up in the body, it results in over-hydration that causes sodium and electrolytes to become too diluted and plummet to life-threatening levels—a condition called hyponatremia. Over-hydration can also lead to increased water pressure inside the skull, which can be fatal. And then there is the obvious water-related danger of drowning. They say that a human being can drown in the shallowest water—just an inch or two. And popular wisdom says that it's always the best swimmers who drown.

Indeed, Warrior Yemaya can use water in many ways to project her power. The hypnotic effect of water on the windshield of a car or on the road while we drive is responsible for countless crashes. As much as the water goddess loves us, she also does not hesitate to remind us of our mortality when she is provoked or disrespected. And yet we continue to bait and provoke her warrior aspects by polluting, over-fishing, and destroying her sacred kingdom. When the healing waters no longer care to heal us because of our abuse, we will only be able to watch as she comes to call, seeking justice and retribution in the form of tidal waves, tsunamis, floods, and—with the help of her sister Oya—hurricanes. In times of great anger, Yemaya delivers the infinite depths of the oceans to Oya, goddess of storms, to spin and churn in spirals of destruction.

What Yemaya gives, she may also take away. That includes not only her compassion, harmony, and healing, but also her gift of life itself. Just as her tides may wash blessings up to you, those blessings can just as easily be pulled back into the ocean depths. And, as the tide turns, we can just as easily be pulled back into the Mother's womb.

Ibu Okunté

One of the most powerful warrior aspects of Yemaya is Ibu Okunté. To understand her, we have to go back a long time in the mysteries of the goddess—back to the aftermath of her rape by her son, Ogun.

When the world was new, the great Mother, Yembo, was raped by her hot-headed son, Ogun. The psychic backlash of this event and Yembo's outrage caused her to split into two distinct beings— Yemaya, who became the Ocean Mother, and Nana Buruku, who ascended to the moon, where she gazes down on humanity wherever her silvery light touches. And while Yemaya eventually softened to Ogun and found some forgiveness and even love for him, Nana Buruku did not, and forever forbade the presence of either Ogun or his metal in her realm.

After her husband, Obatala, abandonned Yemaya, she nervously paced the floors of her palace day after day, unable to forget about Ogun's assault and unable to think of anything else. But something was different now. The goddess fell prey to feelings she did not understand. Although she feared for her safety, she couldn't stop remembering Ogun's dominance and the strength of his embrace. She dwelt on how passionately he had kissed her, how forcefully he had taken control of her body, and how primal their sexual encounter had been. All these memories awakened emotions and feelings deep beneath the surface—feelings hidden so deep that she herself had never known them.

Yemaya decided that she had to find out why she had these feelings, so she left her palace and went off in search of Ogun, who lived in the forest. She searched for days and finally came upon him at his anvil, where he worked hidden far away from the eyes of mankind. When Ogun saw her, his heart overflowed with excitement and love; his eyes lit up with passion and he rushed to embrace her. Although he had thought himself madly in love with Oya, goddess of wind and storms, all thoughts of her were washed away by the Ocean Mother's caress. She taught him the art of loving, and he satisfied her need for passion and lust.

Then Yemaya transformed into a warrior aspect of herself—Okunté—whose prowess in battle nearly exceeded Ogun's. She took to working at Ogun's forge and became as proficient at his art as he, if not more so. To symbolize their shared power, she forged a chain to wear around her waist that held Ogun's sacred tools and they traveled into battle together and reveled in it. As Ibu Okunté, Yemaya loves the heat of battle and the raging emotions that fuel it.

False Priestesses

The warrior aspects of Yemaya do not suffer insults lightly, and her punishments can be imposed far more rapidly than her blessings when she has had enough of bad behavior. One example of this is a story I have retold over the past few years as a cautionary tale.

A witch who had the ear of the Wiccan community had disparaged practitioners of African Traditional Religions for years, even going as far as to express her viewpoint in writing. After years of this criticism, these traditions—and especially Voodoo—became a rising trend in the town in which she owned a shop. And she, like many others, decided to capitalize on their popularity. She created a section of her shop that she called a "House of Voodoo" and commissioned a huge painting of Yemaya to display there. It wasn't long before the store flooded.

Now, for all I know, the actions of this witch were well-meant and maybe even heartfelt. And perhaps if she had formally apologized to the spirit she had insulted or made an offering to her (although she probably would have had to make several), this story might have had a decidedly happier ending. Whatever the case, the sea goddess made her disapproval and her power crystal clear.

Another Wiccan once came to me seeking to learn about the Ocean Mother. The woman seemed so genuine and earnest in her quest that I decided to take her on as a student, even though many concerned peers advised me not to trust her. I would swiftly learn to regret this decision, whose consequences have returned over and over to haunt me.

After taking a brief introductory class with me, this woman managed to convince everyone around her that she was now a priestess of Yemaya—which, in and of itself, would have been blasphemous enough. But this "wanna-blessed-be" then decided that *she* would start teaching people what she had learned from me, as well as a mish-mash of spurious ideas she had cobbled together and made up on her own. With no real formal training, no understanding or respect for practices or tradition, she then created social-media pages where she marketed herself on the Internet to unsuspecting seekers as "the real deal." To make matters even worse, she bad-mouthed *actual* practitioners. Since no one seemed to question her credentials, she continued in her arrogant ways.

One day, this sham priestess allowed her dog to eat from an altar that she had haphazardly erected to Yemaya. Now, this was just the limit to what the sea goddess would stand for. Allowing a dog to desecrate the goddess's offerings was a massive offense to Yemaya because of her ingrained dislike of canines. But this demented devotee did not apologize, or make an offering, or try to appease or assuage the goddess in any other way. She merely justified her ignorance by saying something that I, personally, could not believe I actually heard: "It's okay because Yemaya loves all animals and would never punish a doggie." Goddess only knows in what deluded world she picked up *that* little bit of nonsensical New Age dribble! In a very important story it was a dog who betrayed Yemaya while she hid the divination system she stole from Orula beneath her skirts, the dog bit at her hem and tore the skirt exposing the theft. In retaliation Yemaya beheaded the dog and would never allow dogs around her again.

Well, as sure as it is hot in July, within days the dog became deathly ill, although it did survive. Yet this whacky Wiccan still did nothing to appeal to Yemaya's compassion or forgiveness. Instead, blissfully ignorant, she continued to sell her own false magic and rituals to the unwary. This time, however, Warrior Yemaya did not overlook her misguided actions, but decided to punish them with fire and water. The woman's home was flooded with several inches of water, which encouraged a thick black mold to invade its walls and start an electrical fire that eventually destroyed it. I wish I could say that this arrogant fool eventually learned her lesson, but sadly I cannot. Nor can I think of a single practice of Yemaya that she did not disrespect or a single taboo she did not break. The gods and goddesses of these traditions are *very* set in their ways.

PART II

Yemaya in Myth and Legend

CHAPTER 6

Story Time with Uncle Raven

This is what my friends and students like to call it when I tell the old sacred stories of my spiritual family. I believe this started a few years ago when a close friend began to refer to me as Uncle Raven, although for the life of me I have never been able to figure out why. But I kind of like it and it stuck, so let's enjoy some story time

Most African Traditional Religions are oral traditions, meaning that the stories, practices, and culture are passed on by word of mouth from family member to family member, down through generations. As such they change, sometimes in small ways and sometimes in major ways, although the underlying message or moral of the story stays the same. Because of this, many stories in their modern form are unrecognizable when compared to the original. In the Western hemisphere, this is less true because these communities practice in "houses" that are somewhat like churches and in groups that are somewhat like covens—but that is a very loose analogy.

In oral traditions, the spoken word is more revered than the written word. In these traditions, there are no grand grimoires or ancient stone tablets, no bibles or books of shadows containing sacred stories.

Instead, the fables, parables, and cautionary tales of these traditions are continually retold with fresh voices and from fresh perspectives. Thus they evolve over time and adapt to their social environment, gaining more relevance for the wave of younger students coming up to carry on the priesthood, the religion, and the myths belonging to the orishas. *Patakis* (legends) and parables are recited at nearly every gathering and ceremony in my family; they become bedtime stories, allegories, and cautionary tales. I have seen these stories come to life in movies and even comic books, believe it or not.

I consider the telling of these tales an essential part of being a teacher, and it is my favorite thing to do with my family and friends. In fact, I always wanted to be a storyteller, and I try to pass on stories through my art and poetry. I love this part of my teaching, because it allows me to add my voice to the ancestral choir singing the praise songs of our spiritual devotions. It helps me to embellish the rich tapestry of our mythos and beliefs. It encourages me to become a part of living history and to keep magic alive. Although I don't usually deviate too far from the central concept of the stories I tell, I relate them in my own language with my own accent, and give them my own spin. Sometimes you may find my wording a bit vulgar or clumsy. Sometimes you may find it overly modernized. But I truly believe that the original messages of the tales remain clear and true.

So my dears, why don't you take a comfortable seat with a cool drink, and perhaps settle down with a cozy throw or put a fat purring cat on your lap, and listen to what the spirits and Uncle Raven are layin' down for you.

Late for Dinner

One of my favorite stories shows how humility and respect gain more than greed and selfishness. And how sometimes being fashionably late actually makes for the best entrance.

From the time that time began—and perhaps even longer ago than that—Olodumare had been worshipped as the supreme creator god. It was he who bore the responsibility for everything, including watching over his children, the orishas. But over the many many long years, Olodumare became weary of being tied down to one planet in one universe, even if it was his universe and the planet he had created. He could see that his children had grown in years and wisdom (some much more than others). So, after pondering the situation for a long time, he decided it was time to move on.

When Olodumare decided to leave to start life on other worlds in other universes, he resolved to divide his power over this world among his seven oldest children—Obatala, Ogun, Shango, Oshun, Oya, Eleggua, and Yemaya. So he sent them all invitations to a feast at his palace. They all came quickly, eager to find out what power they would receive. All, that is, except Yemaya, the spirit of the sea. She stayed away.

Olodumare had laid out a sumptuous feast. The long table was covered in white satin and piled high with the most lavish dishes, exotic fruits, and tantalizing treats. But he would not allow the spirits to begin eating until Yemaya arrived. The other orishas sat growing hungry and irritable, knowing that their father would not bestow his powers on them until after dinner. Ogun and Shango began to argue, as the brothers always did when put in proximity for too long. Oshun sat sweetly humming away, daydreaming. Oya and Eleggua grumbled that Yemaya was taking too long to come and that Olodumare shouald go ahead without her. After all, she was quite late by this time—late enough to be insulting and down-right rude. Olodumare refused their requests and insisted that they wait.

When Yemaya's invitation arrived, she was busy sacrificing a ram (her favorite meat). Once she was finished, she found a giant abalone shell and placed the animal's head in the center of it, then surrounded the head with pearls the size of goose eggs, sunken gold pieces, beautiful shells, and corals. She then put on her most exquisite gown of crystal-blue waters and adorned herself with many strings of glowing white pearls and coral beads. She removed her headwrap and let her ebony tresses cascade like a waterfall down to her waist. Upon them, she set her sparkling royal headdress, with white and blue beaded chains dangling fringe-like across her beautiful face. No queen, spirit, or goddess had ever looked finer or more regal than the Mother of All Life did at that moment. She gathered up her offering and went to the surface of her kingdom. There, she rose into the clouds and traveled wrapped in the rain to Olodumare's palace.

In the meantime, Olodumare had grown weary of listening to his children complain and agreed to start dinner. They ate and drank quickly, longing to be done with the seemingly endless delay that Yemaya was causing. When Yemaya finally entered the dining room, all the sounds of feasting died as each of the assembled orishas was struck breathless by her appearance. The majesty of her had never been more clear.

Yemaya approached Olodumare and placed her offering before him. Then she knelt at his feet and asked that she be forgiven for her tardiness. She explained that she did not want to arrive empty-handed and that it had taken some time to put her gift together. "Baba," she said, "forgive my lateness. I worked extremely hard on making this offering suitable for your holy hands to receive."

Olodumare forgave her and asked her to sit and eat, realizing then that there were merely scraps and the head of a fish left. Her greedy relatives had consumed everything else. Yemaya sat proudly at the table, however, glowing and radiant in her royal finery. Without complaint, she took the fish head and ate it. When she had finished, Olodumare rose from his seat.

"My children," he said, "you all came here in your arrogance with empty hands reaching out only to receive and not to give. You worried only about yourselves. You thoughtlessly left almost nothing for your Mother to eat. I am disappointed in you."

He then turned to Yemaya and said: "Of all my children, only you came bearing a gift, the ram's head, and you were rewarded with only a fish's head to eat. But now you will become a head, placed forever above the rest. You will have dominion over the sea, the moon, and the earth. You will be *Oni Ocuny*, the Thrice-Crowned Queen above Queens. You will have access to all of my power, while the rest will receive a far smaller portion. People of all nations will love and honor you for all the days to come."

He then placed the triple crown on her head. The other spirits were, of course, ashamed and offered apologies and asked for forgiveness, which Yemaya, smiling sweetly, gave to all of them.

The First Gift

This story tells of our infatuation with the sound of the ocean waves and its mesmerizing rhythm that soothes and lulls us. These sounds and rhythms are reminiscent of our experience in the womb, and are symbolized by the sweet siren call of the mermaid goddess. Our fascination with water and the comfort it conveys thus reflects our deep desire to stay connected to the source of our birth, the Mother of All Life.

Long ago, when the world was fresh and new and mankind had not long been in it, Yemaya spent much time among her children, singing them sweet songs of motherly love. The children passed many hours enraptured by these songs and entranced by their mother's singing—so much so that they began to turn away from their work and responsibilities to the kingdom. Crops went uncared for, withering and dying in the hot sun. The marketplace was empty; no one manned the forge or hunted. Houses fell into shambles, and the elderly and the very young were left to fend for themselves. Live-stock went unattended, unfed, or unwatered and, like the crops, they began to die.

Worst of all, however, the rituals and ceremonies performed for other spirits were being ignored, as were the spirits themselves. This generated a low current of discontent among these neglected orishas that rumbled like thunder among them, and they went to Obatala, Father of the World, to complain. "Baba," they began, "we love our Mother Yemaya above all things, but the humans have turned away from us. Our ceremonies are no longer performed; our offerings are not being made. The crops and cattle go uncared for and no work is being done. The beauty of the earth is fading because her children cannot turn away from Yemaya's song. It possesses and holds them in rapture and no one can resist her sway."

Obatala thought long and hard about this. Clearly, it was unfair that humanity was ignoring the other spirits. And it was certainly unacceptable for no work to be done on the farms and in the fields. It was disgraceful that the elderly and the very young were left to care for themselves, and that the houses were falling into disrepair. So he summoned Yemaya to his palace. She arrived surrounded by a crowd of people who were made, quite unhappily, to wait outside.

"Radiant queen of the sea, earth, and moon, beloved bringer of life, bearer of celestial light," Obatala began, "I have called you on behalf of the other spirits, your first-born children. They are upset and hurt by the way mankind has abandoned all else in favor of your songs. It is unfair to them and to the kingdom, which lies in waste, that your children should care only for the sound of your voice. So I have decided that you must return to your home under the sea until they are ready to hear your songs *and* attend to the kingdom and its needs."

Yemaya's beautiful face became a mask of concern and sadness. "But I cannot leave them without a mother," she protested, "without a mother's voice to comfort and sooth them."

"It is decided, oh Queen," Obatala responded. "I know in your wisdom that you will find a way to be there for them without being there among them."

Yemaya realized that the decision was final and that Obatala was extending her a courtesy by explaining the reasoning behind it. So she resigned herself to taking his advice and committed herself to finding a way to resolve the problem. She swam to her palace of coral and mother of pearl and began to search for the solution.

Meanwhile, on the land, Yemaya's children sank into a deep depression. Without their mother's songs, they became even more uninterested in their responsibilities. It seemed that the world would surely not survive.

But deep beneath the waves, the Mother of All Life had an epiphany. She found a large conch shell and, holding it to her lips, began to sing into it, filling its chambers with her magical voice. When the shell was full, she returned to the surface, carrying it with her. She brought the shell to the kingdom of man, telling her children: "In times of loneliness or sadness, when you most need my comfort, when you need to be reminded of my love for you—but only when your work is done—put this shell to your ears and you will hear me singing to you." With that, she vanished back into the sea.

And this is why, to this day, we hear the sound of the ocean in seashells—as a reminder of Yemaya's first gift to mankind.

Too Many Cooks

There are many stories in which Yemaya is involved in an abusive relationship, the most famous being that of her rape by Ogun, god of iron and progress. Here is a somewhat lesser-known tale.

For a time when Yemaya was married to Ogun, they lived very happily in his forest home, spending their time making love and working toward the betterment and evolution of mankind. Each of them regarded the other with care and consideration for many years. But these two strong personalities living under one roof proved to be a recipe for disaster—which is quite often the case.

Although the beginning their marriage had been happy enough, Yemaya began to grow bored and unhappy living on the surface. So obvious was her lack of joy and her gloomy mood that Ogun, meaning to cheer her up, decided that he would cook her all of her favorite foods in the hope that he would see her radiant smile once again.

Ogun took to the kitchen to begin working. But he was a bit clumsy and unfamiliar with the culinary arts because someone else had always cooked for him and waited on him. In fact, he had never cooked anything before, and had never even seen the inside of a kitchen. Not long into his preparations, he accidentally dropped Yemaya's favorite tureen. It hit the floor and shattered into many pieces. Hearing the crash, Yemaya rushed to see what had happened. When she saw her cherished pottery destroyed, the white and blue shards scattered everywhere, she chastised her husband, calling him clumsy and careless.

At first, Ogun was hurt. Had he not been trying to please her? To make her happy? Who was she to come at him with such arrogance? Then hurt turned to rage and, in his anger, the god of iron struck Yemaya's beautiful face. She fell to the floor in pain and shock, feeling the horror that comes from such an act of violence. But within moments, she began to rise like the tide, swelling and growing until she seemed to engulf the entire dwelling.

"How dare you?" she scolded. "How dare you lay a hand on your wife?" Her crystal tears fell like rain, filling the house with salt water and submerging Ogun completely, until it seemed sure that he would drown. Yemaya left him then, and the water receded. But as it did, it took half of Ogun's power with it, leaving him less strong than he had been in retribution for his act of violence against her.

And from that day to this, Yemaya has been the advisor and deliverer of women in abusive relationships and victims of men's violence.

The Perils of Lust

Shortly after his arrival on earth, Shango, the orisha of thunder and lightning, was given to Yemaya to foster. Having never known his biological mother, Shango grew up to know only Yemaya in that role. When he came of age, he left his mother's *ilé* (house) and went out into the world, becoming a raging, misogynistic, womanizing playboy, forgetting all about Yemaya and failing to respect women in general.

After more than a few years had passed, Shango came back to the kingdom of the orishas to attend an important party being thrown by Obatala, the king of the spirits, at his palace by the sea. Everyone who was anyone was there, drinking and dancing and singing. Shango quickly became intoxicated and began to beat the drums. His talent for drumming was without equal and everyone began to celebrate him. All the women flirted with him shamelessly—except for one.

This woman was the most beautiful creature he had ever set eyes on. Her hair was loose, cascading in ebony waves to her waist, and was adorned with glowing deep-sea pearls and tiny glittering crystals. Her caramel skin glistened as if with dew and her eyes, which shifted colors continuously, seemed almost hypnotic to him. Her blue gown was as sheer as water and barely contained the glory of her body. And though her lips never parted, Shango could swear he heard her singing over the cacophony of the party.

As his lust for her swelled, however, Shango noticed that she was *not* noticing him. But how could that be? He was the most handsome of all the orishas, and all women fell for his erotic charms. Didn't they?

The mystery woman stood and began to dance slowly and sensually. Her hips undulated with the rhythm of the drums; her arms moved serpent-like as she danced. Her exotic perfume swirled about her in the air, making it heavy and sultry, ever more intoxicating, until Shango began to sweat. He licked his lips like a wolf stalking a deer. He had to have her—now! He danced over to her and began to mirror her sexy movements.

"I am Shango, ruler of thunder and fire," he said, as their hips bucked in syncopated rhythm.

"I know who you are," she replied. "But clearly you don't remember me."

"We have never met, Lady," he said, "for if we had, I could never have forgotten such a magnificent creature. I must have you." He grabbed the woman's small waist and pulled her to him, leaning in to kiss her. But she pushed him back.

"Oh my king," she whispered flirtatiously, "I want you too, but not here in front of all these gossips. My house is not far from here. Let's go there, where we can continue this dance in privacy."

Shango agreed and they quickly left the party. The woman led him down the beach to the shore, where a little silvery boat awaited them. She stepped into the boat and beckoned for him to do the same. Now, although Shango was mighty indeed, he hated the water because he did not know how to swim. But his desire and the swelling in his pants overwhelmed that fear and he got into the boat. As soon as he did, the boat began to drift farther and farther out into the open water, until he could no longer see the shore.

"Where is your house, woman?" Shango bellowed. She assured him that it was just a little farther and shot him a look that nearly froze his heart. The waves started to become choppy and a violent storm began brewing in the sky. The boat rocked and threatened to tip over. Then the mystery woman that Shango had lusted after all night dove off the boat and vanished in the waves. The sea churned and crashed and the waves grew taller and taller. As Shango's panic grew, a great tidal wave appeared and hung in the air above him. Shango cried out in fear for mercy.

Then he saw her, glowing with supernatural light standing on top of the wave—the angry goddess of the sea, the Ocean Mother.

"Ungrateful child," she shouted, "how dare you seek to disrespect me, of all the women in the world?" Her voice pounded in his ears louder than the surf. The wave began to descend and threatened to swallow him whole, until her face loomed directly above his own. Clearly, she was holding the water back. "Are you still such an arrogant, disrespectful pig of a man that you do not recognize me?" Her teeth gnashed as she scolded.

"*Enough!*" Obatala's voice rang through the storm-tossed sky. "Shango, you have forgotten your mother!"

Tears welled up in Yemaya's eyes and her anger softened, as all anger does in the pacifying light of Obatala's presence.

"My king," Shango replied, "my mother abandoned me as an infant."

"No, Shango. Although that may be true, it was she, Yemaya, the Mother of All Life, who raised you at my request. It was she who provided for you and cared for you with her motherly loving ways. Yet despite this, you sought tonight to defile her." A look of shock twisted Shango's face. His shame spilled out of his eyes as tears of regret.

"*Omi o,*" Shango cried, "please forgive me. I am ashamed and humbled. I would never have disrespected you. I do not know how I could have forgotten you, my mother. Great Queen above Queens, forgive your wayward son."

And with that, the waters became calm and shining once again, and the sky became peaceful and quiet. Once more, Yemaya, the most beautiful creature Shango had ever seen, stood on the boat with her arms outstretched to embrace him. She gave him a nod of forgiveness and a smile that could melt ice and soothe the soul, for there is no anger or rage stronger than a mother's love. Shango never again disrespected Yemaya, but from that day until this, Shango fears only two things: the dead and Yemaya's wrath.

The chemistry and tension between Shango and Yemaya remained, however. Although she had raised him, Shango was not her biological son. And although their mutual attraction was never acted upon, it remained evident whenever they were seen together.

Sibling Rivalry

This is a tale of the rivalry that often occurs between siblings and how it can disrupt the harmony of family relationships—or peace in the wider community. It also shows how this rivalry can create rifts in families and in society unless wisdom and justice work together to restore balance.

Oya, goddess of wind and storms, had fallen madly and passionately in love with Shango, the womanizing god of thunder and lightning. At that time, he was married to his only legitimate wife, Obba, the goddess of devotion, who doted on him and took care of his every need. She cleaned for him and cooked for him. But nothing she did could stop his wandering eye and whoring ways. Oya decided to take advantage of this and sought counsel from her sister, Yemaya.

Oya traveled to Yemaya's kingdom beneath the sea, where she found her holding court. Seated on a throne of coral and mother of pearl and surrounded by her sirens, Yemaya was going over the needs of the kingdom. She was thrilled to see her little sister and rushed to embrace her. She offered her a seat beside the throne and asked what news she had from the land above, and why she had come to visit.

Oya explained that she desired to win Shango away from their other sister, Obba, but that she wasn't quite sure how to go about it. She had come to enlist Yemaya's aid. The goddess of the sea listened to Oya's story with a heaviness in her heart. Then she explained that, while she understood and had compassion for Oya, Obba was also her sister and Shango her adopted son. As such, she could not become involved and could not help her. She had to remain neutral in this matter.

Oya flew into a rage, driven, as she often was, by her unbridled passion. She exclaimed that, if anyone else had come to her with a similar request, Yemaya would have helped and that she was being treated unfairly. But Yemaya maintained her position. Oya left and later, in another version of the tale, sought out Oshun, her youngest sister, who indeed did help her betray Obba—albeit with ulterior motives—and win Shango. Oya harbored resentment for Yemaya after that, and most of their trouble would forever be centered on Shango.

In the Americas, there is a popular notion that Yemaya and Oya hate each other, but this is not completely true. There are modern stories about Yemaya tricking Oya into living in the graveyard so that she could take the sea from her. This tale, as far as I have ever been able to discover, is not in any way traditional. Nor have I ever seen or heard this tale—or any even remotely similar to it—in my own training or research.

There are simply too many stories of Yemaya and Oya working together to support that notion. Moreover, Yemaya gives her waters to Oya to create the hurricane, her strongest weapon. I have been told by many initiates of the orisha traditions practicing in Africa that they have never heard that these two spirits hate each other or cannot be served at the same table. Air and water are both necessary to maintain life and they work together to do so. Do Yemaya and

Oya argue? Of course. Show me two sisters who never argue, and I'll show you at least one sister who is not telling the truth.

Sisterly Love

This story, by contrast, is about the devotion of sisters, and the way that family members take care of each other. It is also a shining example of how Yemaya, in her love and great compassion, can heal even the darkest depression.

There was a time long ago when the joyous Oshun, goddess of love and attraction, was not so very joyous. In fact, she had fallen on hard times and fled from the kingdom in shame, taking with her only the white dress she was wearing. She ran and ran until she reached a river and, throwing herself onto its bank, wept and wept for weeks. Her white dress turned a dingy off-white. And, to top it all off, her glorious long hair began falling out in clumps due to her stress and worry.

Oshun didn't know it, but the spirit of the river carried her tears to the sea, where they told Yemaya of her little sister's pain and plight. Finally, the Ocean Mother decided it was time to intervene on her sister's behalf.

Yemaya appeared on the banks of the river where Oshun lay, miserable and balding and aged beyond her years. Her dirty dress was stained with tears. Yemaya's heart broke when she laid her crystal eyes on her beloved sister. She helped Oshun to her feet and wiped her tears away with the hem of her voluminous skirts, then kissed her sweetly on her forehead, restoring youth and beauty to her face. Next, she swept up all the gold the river could carry from the sea and laid it at her sister's feet. "You will never be poor again," she declared, "for I have given you all the world's gold—and not just what I have brought here. This abundance will never run out."

Then Yemaya placed her hand on the disgraceful dress her sister had been forced to wear every day, and, in a flash, the fabric turned a vivid glowing yellow, which from that day on would be Oshun's color. But Yemaya was far from finished. Seeing her sister's baldness, she twisted her own cascading hair, which nearly swept the ground, into a ponytail and cut it in half. The severed locks became a wig that Oshun could wear until her own hair grew back. The light of happiness beamed once again from the golden goddess' eyes.

Next Yemaya gave Oshun a fan (a symbol of status) and a mirror that would always reflect the inner beauty of anyone who gazed into it. She summoned a peacock, which had long been Yemaya's favorite bird, and gave the dazzling creature, with all its associations with royalty, to her youngest sister. Oshun was restored and elevated by her sister's gifts and overcome by her generosity and love, which cemented their bond for all eternity.

"One last thing," Yemaya said, placing an ornate golden crown decorated with river pearls and cowrie shells on top of Oshun's head. "You left as a queen, sister, and as a queen you will return to the world." Oshun never suffered again, and Yemaya became the spirit of compassion. And from that day until this, wherever Yemaya goes, Oshun goes with her.

The Price of Betrayal

This story is of the snitches-get-stitches variety. It is a cautionary tale about involving yourself in other people's marital or relationship troubles. It also demonstrates how throwing someone else under the bus in order to take the heat off yourself often results in more trouble for you anyway. There are many versions of this story; here is mine.

One day, Yemaya decided to steal the secret of divination from her husband at that time, Orunmila, the god of prophecy. He was often gone for weeks to see clients in other kingdoms, leaving the easily bored Yemaya alone. She studied his practice of *Obi* (the traditional use of cowrie shells to communicate with the spirits) when he wasn't aware of her, memorizing all of the meanings of all the combinations of shells and how they fell (see chapter 11). She studied every moment of every day that her husband was away and she practiced every day in secret while he was at home. The clever goddess was careful not to let him catch her watching, however, pretending to be doing household chores while observing every throw and every interpretation he made. She listened to all the advice her husband gave his clients and all the *ebbos* (major formal offerings based on what the mouths of the shells suggest) that he told them to perform (see chapter 11).

When the time finally came for Orunmila to go on another journey, he kissed his wife goodbye and departed, leaving Yemaya to put into practice all she had learned. She prepared her shells the way she had seen him do a thousand times; she swept the floor, laid down the mat, burned sacred herbs, and purified the house. Finally, everything seemed ready. As Orunmila's clients began to arrive, expecting the diviner to be at home, they were greeted by his beautiful wife instead.

Yemaya began consulting the shells for those of her husband's clients who could not wait for his return. All the people who came to her remarked that she was a better reader than Orunmila because of her compassionate manner. At first, this delighted her. But then she realized that, when he returned, her husband would not be pleased. So she told everyone who came that she would not be available to consult the shells for them until Orunmila left again. They all agreed to keep her readings secret.

When Orunmila returned, Yemaya carried on business as usual, although she may have seemed too attentive to her husband and perhaps sweeter than usual. After a few days at home, Orunmila became suspicious. Yemaya's improved disposition and the fact that he seemed to have fewer and fewer new clients coming to see him seemed a curious coincidence to him. And almost none of his regular customers were coming at all. As he thundered around the house, Yemaya grew more and more frightened for her safety.

Eventually, there was a knock at the door and, to Orunmila's delight and Yemaya's dismay, one of his regular clients stood before him. When Yemaya saw him, she realized that he was the *only* client she had not sworn to secrecy about her readings. She silently started packing a bag with her shells, jewels, and gowns, making ready to flee at a moment's notice should the need arise.

When the smiling god of prophecy asked how he could serve his client, the man replied that he would rather see Yemaya, who was even better at reading the shells than he was. At that, the smiling god ceased smiling. He flew into a rage, screaming for his wife, who had already escaped out the back door and run as far and as fast as her feet could carry her. As she fled, she ran past the duck Kuekueye, nearly knocking him over. Kuekueye ruffled his feathers in protest as she flew past him paying him no mind. Yemaya escaped into the forest where Iroko, the spirit of the ceiba tree, sheltered her within his branches for days. The grumpy Kuekueye, non-plussed by Yemaya's apparent rudeness, decided to follow her into the forest. Seeing her take refuge in the tree, he committed her hiding place to memory.

Meanwhile, Orunmila searched night and day for his wife. But it was no use; no matter how long he searched or how far he traveled, the elusive goddess of the sea could simply not be found. He even searched for her in her underwater kingdom, only to return home unsuccessful. The angry diviner finally gave up the search after nine long weeks.

With Yemaya gone, Orunmila's home fell into disarray. Without her there to cook her incomparably delicious meals, he found himself seriously hungry and decided that he would have to fend for himself. His pride, however, would not allow him to set foot in the marketplace, because too many people had heard of Yemaya's betrayal and flight. Since he did not wish to be looked on with pity or gossiped about as he walked by, he decided he would go hunting instead. He borrowed a bow and arrows from Ochossi, the god of hunting, and set off into the forest to find his prey.

Not long after he left for the forest, Orunmila came upon Kuekueye, who was wandering aimlessly as ducks are prone to do. Orunmila drew his bow and prepared to launch an arrow through the duck's heart, but stopped in shock when Kuekueye began to beg for mercy saying: "Do not kill me, oh king. I have the answer that you have sought day and night all over the land. If you kill me now, that answer dies along with me and you will never find your wife. I know where she hides." The duck swelled with pride and self-satisfaction, impressed by his own cleverness. He had managed to save his own life and also get some revenge on the careless goddess who had nearly trampled him in the woods.

Taken aback by this, Orunmila agreed to spare the duck. Tucking Kuekueye under his arm, he followed his directions through the twisting forest, over rivers, and through thickets, until he came to the ceiba tree that had protected Yemaya and kept her hidden from him. In his anger at discovering his estranged wife in the foliage, the orisha of prophecy and divination threw his shells at her. They landed on the ground at Iroko's roots. He bellowed at Yemaya, turning red in the face and gnashing his teeth.

Because she had stolen them from him, Orunmila exclaimed, he would never again throw the shells—completely overlooking the fact that, if he were a bit less prideful, together he and Yemaya could have doubled their clientele and their income. Instead, he raged on that she could keep the shells, which were now "tainted," and that he would craft a new way to divine—a table of divination that no woman in the world, goddess or mortal, would ever be allowed to use. Then he divorced his wife on the spot and stormed back home, leaving Yemaya and Kuekueye alone.

But things were about to take a very serious turn for the duck. The air all around Yemaya became filled with down-pouring rain, her hair streaming upward in the wind as her head wrap unraveled and fell to the forest floor. Her eyes darkened and flashed like a storm at sea. The duck heard the violent crashing of waves and the sacred rhythms of drums thundering in the distance. Yemaya's slender arms grew thicker and more muscular. Her legs grew together into a scaley, coiling sea serpent's tail and a great scimitar appeared at her waist as she took on her warrior aspect. Her voice echoed in the air as she admonished the water fowl.

"Foolish, selfish duck," the goddess cried. "How dare you betray the mother who granted you and all living things life? To save yourself, you conspired against me." Then she raised the scimitar above her head and said: "From now on I will eat your flesh and the flesh of your descendants."

Grabbing the terrified duck, Yemaya tore out all his feathers, which she would fashion into a fan. Ignoring all of his cries for mercy, she lopped off his head, drank his blood, and devoured his flesh. "You should have minded your own business," she said. Then she vanished in a spray of salt water, returning to her palace at the bottom of the sea.

This may have been the first time in history that someone was killed for meddling in the affairs of another. But it wouldn't be the last.

Bittersweet Parting

This next story is based on the final incarnation of Yemaya. It takes place after Yemaya's short-lived marriage to Arganu, when she becomes *Omi Leto*, the axis upon which the world turns. In this story about her life on earth and the end of the lives of all the orishas on earth, Yemaya transitions into Ibu Agana, the Mother of All Life.

The kingdom of the orishas began when Yemaya, as Yembo, met and fell in love with Oko, the god of agriculture, then known as Oddua. Many centuries after the orishas first set foot upon the earth, Yemaya and Oko met again. Once again, the two fell deeply in love. They were two soulmates who had been separated by many reincarnations. And just as the orishas' time on earth had begun with Yemaya and Oko's love, the end of their time on earth was heralded by their reunion. But the final days of the kingdom would be days of peace.

Yemaya and Oko shared many happy years filled with love and happiness. They dedicated themselves to their duties and ensured that all wars and conflicts ended. Once they had been successful in this endeavor, they began to visit all the other orishas to let them know that the time to leave the kingdom behind had finally, after many hundreds of years, arrived. Moreover, as they left the kingdom of earth behind, they would have to leave their physical forms behind as well.

Soon after Yemaya and Oko returned to their home, Olodumare appeared to them in a flash of brilliant light and began to speak. "Omi Leto," he began, "the time has come for you to leave this world. But be comforted by knowing that, even in death, you will give birth and continue to be the Mother of All Life. As your physical body dies, you will give birth to the first sixteen humans, who will become the new rulers of the earth. I shall send your children all over the world so that your worship will never die. You will always be *Ony Ocuny*, the Thrice-Crowned Queen above Queens, and remembered for eternity by your children."

Yemaya felt a great swelling in her heart, knowing that she would give birth to the entire human race. This brought her happiness and a sense of purpose that she had never truly felt before. And in that moment, she became Yemaya Ibu Agana, the Mother of All Things.

Yemaya walked out into the middle of the courtyard of the home she and Oko had built and had filled for so many years with love, happiness, and peace. As she stood in the warm glow of golden sunlight, her feet began to tingle. When she looked down, she saw them begin to turn to sand, and watched as the sand scattered in the wind. The transformation continued up her calves and thighs, and, when it reached her rib cage, she felt an explosion of rapture and ecstasy. Her ribs burst forth from her disappearing body and became the first human men and women to walk the earth.

Yemaya smiled as she watched the birth of each of her human children and, before she vanished from the earth, was content in the knowledge that her children would now multiply and populate the entire planet. They would have children, who would have children, and so on until the end of the universe, and she would never be forgotten. She was secure in the confidence that her name would be glorified forever. And when the spirits of all the orishas ascended into the heavens, Yemaya took her place at the center of the universe.

Smell the Roses

Despite the previous tale, it has been said that the orishas continue to manifest in physical form even now, in modern times. And I have experienced this on more than one occasion. It always seems to happen during a time of spiritual or emotional struggle in my life. This nontraditional tale, which is close to my heart, tells of how I met the Ocean Mother on my street.

This one particular Sunday morning, I was sitting on the front porch of a house that my husband and I had rented after being evicted from an apartment owned by a couple for whom I had worked. I had left their employ after becoming aware of some shady dealings there. It was only a few days after my brother's suicide when these people informed me that we had to move out. I was blown away by the insensitivity they showed me, as we had been relatively close. Although I no longer worked for them, I still paid my rent and they knew what I was going through. Only days before, they had sat on the back porch of their house with me and told me how sorry they were for the loss of my brother.

Well, we moved to a pretty little blue-and-white home in a quiet neighborhood. And as I sat there on my new front porch staring out at nothing, I found myself lost in doubts and insecurities regarding my future. I worried that I would have to go back to reading tarot cards out of my kitchen—something that I really didn't want to do and that was far from a guaranteed paycheck. There were no other metaphysical shops in my area where I could work, and the serious health problems I was dealing with at the time made it impossible for me to go back into the restaurant industry, which had been my profession for many years. Needless to say, I was pretty scared.

All of this bad news had manifested over the weekend of Yemaya and Oshun's feast days—September 7th and 8th—a period that I had anticipated would be a time of happiness and celebration, This left me feeling confused and shaken. Why would this be the way that the goddess to whom I had devoted my entire life chose to celebrate with me?

I stared blankly as tears rolled down my cheeks and fell like rain drops to the floor. I was all alone in this new house with far too much time on my hands to become immersed in my own feelings. And so I did. I let myself go and sank deeply into them. As I wallowed in my own doubts, the sun began to climb higher in the late-morning sky and a cool autumn-like breeze brought what I swear was the smell of salt water, roses, and watermelon. I had planted roses in the yard, so that explained that scent, but not the others. I looked all around, trying to discern where the other aromas were coming from.

And then I saw them. Two beautiful, dark-skinned women I had never seen in the neighborhood before were walking down my street. The two ladies appeared to be dressed for church in beautiful dresses and giant hats. The older woman had long dark braids that fell to her waist; her dress and hat were the color of a clear blue sky and her smile was brilliant. The younger woman wore her hair loose to her shoulders and was clothed in the color of a glorious summer day—a golden yellow that seemed to shine with its own light. They walked with their arms linked, talking and laughing as they made their way past my yard. They stopped and smelled the roses I had planted in honor of Yemaya and my mother who had passed away—white roses for the goddess and yellow roses for my mom, as they had been her favorites (and Oshun's as well). I distinctly remember thinking that I heard the woman in blue whispering to the flowers.

"Take some," I called out to her. She smiled, thanked me, and plucked one white and one yellow rose from my garden. She put the white rose behind her ear, where it glowed like the moon at midnight against her ebony braids. She handed the yellow rose to her companion, who placed it in her cleavage. As they passed out of my view, I heard them laughing and talking again. And this time I could have sworn I heard the lady in blue say: "For all things, there is a reason"

I stood up quickly, struck by the words and the realization that this had been a visitation from the Mother of All Life and Oshun, the goddess of love. I ran around the corner of my house to get another look at the women, but they were gone, leaving no trace behind them. Over the next few days, I casually inquired of my neighbors (who must have thought I was a nut) if they knew these ladies. No one had any idea who I was talking about. And I never saw them again.

After that day, I felt the strength of my faith return. I stopped being afraid that I would not be able to make enough money to support my family, and the blue-and-white house became one of the most magical homes I have ever had. But really, the most amazing and magical result of that late-summer visitation, that glorious September morning, was the fact that my roses continued to bloom all through the fall into winter, the last bloom opening on the morning of December 24, Christmas Eve. No one will ever to be able to convince me that was not Yemaya's doing.

In the next few years, I encountered other manifestations of Yemaya on earth. Sometimes I was alone; sometimes I was with my godson or my husband or my best friend, Rob. Regardless of who was with me, however, the magic of these sightings always brought clarity or healing of some kind.

When I tell my students about these happenings, I tell them: "You will see this; it will happen and you will doubt yourself. But don't. You're not crazy; this is real and it's important and it's sacred." Our gods do not hide out in some unknowable, unreachable place. They still walk the earth and interact with us, influencing us and inspiring us, without us even realizing who they are. Well, most of the time anyway.

CHAPTER 7

Eleggua—Trickster, Warrior, Sage

It is impossible to write a book about Yemaya or any of the ori-sha spirits without including information about Eleggua, the god of chance and fate. The role that Eleggua plays in our relationship with Yemaya is particularly important. But before you can understand that role, you must first know a little bit about this orisha.

Eleggua is the keeper of the keys to the gates between the world of mortal men and the world of the orishas. He is the spirit of com-munication and crossroads. The youngest male orisha, he is also one of the most powerful and important because, without him, nothing can happen. Eleggua facilitates or denies all communication with the other gods. If he does not open the way for you, all your prayers, petitions, requests, and pleas will go unheard and thus unanswered. And despite some outsiders claiming that they have been able to reach Yemaya (or any other spirit) without his intercession, or that they have successfully invoked her in their magic or rituals without him opening the door to her, they assuredly have not. While their spells and rituals may have been successful, that success was brought about by their own power and not the Ashé of Yemaya. They may even have been touched briefly by the very outermost part of her energy. But without Eleggua to open the way for them, that is about all the influence she will have had in their work.

Eleggua owns all roads and pathways, all doors and portals. He represents the beginning of all things, as well as the end of them. He is fate and chance, luck and opportunity. He is a trickster who delights in games and mischief. He is fond of causing accidents to make a point or to teach a lesson, and each one can become more and more malicious until the test is passed, the lesson learned, or the point made.

Eleggua is all things and their opposites, as expressed in this praise poem that I wrote to him twenty-seven years ago:

> Eleggua is so big he cannot be seen behind that blade of
> grass.
> Eleggua is so small the whole universe cannot contain him.
> When he arrives, he waves good bye.
> When he departs, he says hello.
> He does not end; he does not begin.
> He has always been.
> He has not been born nor has he died,
> But, in his death, was reborn
> Into the kingdom of the orishas.

Eleggua knows all that has happened, is happening, and is yet to happen. He is an invaluable ally and a fearsome enemy, as he owns all the misfortunes (*osobogos*) of the world and can open the door to Iku (the spirit of death) herself when pushed too far into anger. Eleggua walks the road before us, placing obstacles in our way, and how we deal with them decides whether he will clear the way or add more complications to our path.

Calling on Eleggua

Eleggua is the first spirit called in any ceremony and the last to leave. We make offerings to him before we make offerings to any other spirit. This is accepted practice (see chapter 11). Remember: These spirits have been served in this way since the dawn of their arrival on earth. This is their preferred way to be approached, and this part of our practice is non-negotiable—especially for outsiders. This is not to say that you will not feel Yemaya's presence or her love without Ellegua. But that is the extent of the contact you will be allowed once you begin to worship her unless you involve the keeper of the keys.

I start every prayer to Yemaya with a short supplication to the trickster god:

> Baba Eleggua, open my way to the radiant spirit of Yemaya
> That I may serve and commune with her.
> Ashé Eleggua, Ashé.

Traditionally, devotees keep an image of Eleggua by the entrance to their home—typically a cement head with cowrie-shell eyes. You can easily find one online and in most botanicas. Ask to have it blessed by a practitioner. A lot of store owners in the Afro-Latin community will be able to do it or can suggest someone to you.

Eleggua's colors are black and red. His day of the week is Monday and his sacred numbers are 3 and its multiples. He manifests as a young child (the trickster), a strong beautiful youth (the warrior), and a mature older man (the sage). His offerings include (in all manifestations) black coffee, dark rum, candies, sweets, cakes, cigars, tobacco, keys, small children's toys, male goats, chickens, possum, rats, roosters, black and red feathers, black and red candles, black and red beads, coconuts, and bananas and plantains.

Eleggua can be a glutton and loves to eat. And he must always eat first—even before the Mother of All Life. In the world, Eleggua can be found at all intersections, crossroads, doorways, street corners, and any in-between places, like thresholds. And although these are all his sacred spaces, he is everywhere at once. Eleggua is the omni-sentient incarnation of fate. His role in your relationship with Yemaya will show itself to be invaluable.

Eleggua is similar to Papa Legba in the Voodoo traditions in that they both have a bright and a dark counterpart. For Papa Legba, the darker side is *Met Kalfu*; for Eleggua, the dark of night and its spirits is *Eshu*. Eshu is the extremely chaotic part of Eleggua. Or perhaps it would be more precise to say that the two share a symbiotic relationship. While Eleggua is generally mischievous but benign, Eshu is a dangerous spirit who brings out the more reckless and harmful aspects of Eleggua's tricks. Eshu is kept outside worshippers' houses and given the remains of Eleggua's food offerings to avoid bringing strife and chaos into the home. Some people use their names interchangeably, which can be confusing.

There is far more that can be said about this sacred keeper of the keys. Suffice it here to say that devotion to Yemaya necessarily involves dealing with Eleggua. Tales about his antics and the role he plays in the worship of Yemaya and her spiritual family abound. Here are just a few.

Breach of Contract

After Yemaya had learned the art of divination, she taught her sisters Oya and Oshun the skill. The three then decided to go into business together. They set themselves up in a beautiful hut on the beach, which they decorated with shells and nets of glittering silver, copper, and gold. They stood tall vases of peacock feathers in each corner.

The hut was opulent and breathtaking. Yet despite Yemaya's burgeoning renown as a diviner, the sisters had precious little success. Even Oshun's popularity and Oya's reputation for wise council didn't seem to help.

Eleggua—in his aspect of Eleggua Laroye, the spirit of communication and public relations—decided he would "help" the sisters, but also teach them a lesson about honesty and fairness. He arrived at their hut early on a Monday morning and asked how bussiness was, although he already knew, since Eleggua knows all that is and was and will be. After Yemaya explained their plight, Eleggua agreed to spread the news that they were open for business across the land. "I will bring you more clients than you can handle," he said. "For a price."

"And what do you seek in compensation?" the Ocean Mother inquired.

"Oh not much at all," he replied. "Just one fourth of all that you earn."

The three sisters looked to each other, thought for a moment, and then nodded in agreement.

Eleggua vanished. Within minutes, a line began to form at the door of the hut. Client after client came to seek the sisters' wisdom. All three were kept busy from the time the hut opened until the time that it closed. As Eleggua continued to promote their skills, the sisters' reputation and following grew. And so did their fortune. This continued for many weeks, during which time the sisters held true to the bargan they had struck with him.

But soon, they began to complain about how much of their earnings they had to share with Eleggua. "We do all the work," Oshun lamented. "I work all day and night and he gets as much of the profit as I do"

Oya chimed in, wondering if they still even needed Eleggua's help. "We have a long line of clients everyday," she pointed out.

"Surely our reputation now speaks for itself. How do we really even know if what he is doing is actually having any effect?"

Yemaya looked at her sisters and agreed with them. And then the three sisters hatched a plan. Every week, when Eleggua appeared for his payment, they would give him less and less, claiming that business was going badly, until finally they would stop paying him altogether.

But Eleggua knows all that is and was and will be. So he was immediately aware of the sisters' deceit and he resolved to teach them the lesson he had prepared for them months before. He sat himself down in a chair on the beach, just out of view of the hut. For the next three weeks, he told all who came down the path to the hut that the sisters had gone out of business and were no longer available. After three weeks had passed and their clientele had disappeared, the sisters finally summoned Eleggua to the hut.

"You haven't been doing your job," Oshun protested.

"We have had no clients for almost a month," Oya scowled. "You haven't been keeping your side of our bargain."

Before Yemaya could even add to their complaints, Eleggua's presence swelled until it completely engulfed the room. He looked directly at the sisters and asked ominously: "Have you been keeping yours?"

Oshun, Oya, and Yemaya all looked down in shame. Finally, Yemaya broke the silence.

"We have been false and foolish," she said. "We let greed and pride overcome our better selves. We have wronged you. From this day forward, we will never deceive you again. Each week, you will receive your share of the profits before anyone else gets a share. Furthermore, we will give you what we owe you from before, if you will only forgive us and return our clients and come back to work with us."

Eleggua agreed and, with a sly smile and a snap of his fingers, a line of customers that wound its way for miles down the beach appeared at the door. Eleggua had kept his promise, and the three sisters never broke theirs again.

Trash Treatment

Now it came to pass that Olodumare, the creator of the universe, fell victem to a mysterious illness. He developed a fever that raged higher and higher until he became bed ridden, and this caused a panic among his children, the orishas. They huddled close to their creator's bedside. The supreme god of creation had never been ill before, they worried. What strange forces must be at work to strike him down in this way?

On the first day, Oya, who controls the breath of life, tried to heal Olodumare. She summoned winds thick with healing vapors and cool breezes to soothe the fever. But her attempts failed, and he grew sicker.

On the second day, Oshun, who owns the sweet waters of the world, tried to heal him. She summoned water from all the healing wells and springs of the world to restore him. But her attempts failed, and Olodumare grew sicker.

One the third day, Yemaya Olokun, who owns all the oceans and carries the power to give or take life, tried to heal him. She called forth the very spirits of life, and flooded the air around him with her healing, living waters. But her attempts failed and the creator god grew sicker still.

For the next few days, each of the orishas tried to heal their father.

Obatala, the king of purity, tried to heal him.

Chango, the king of thunder and lightning, tried to heal him.

Oggun, the king of progress and iron, tried to heal him.

Even the miraculous healer Babalue Aye, the owner of all diseases and their cures, tried to restore Olodumare to health. But just as for the others, his attempts failed and Olodumare grew sicker still.

On the eigth day, Eleggua appeared and announced to the others that he would heal Olodumare. The older orishas dismissed him, saying that if the oldest, the wisest, the most powerful, the most skillful, and the most competent healers had all failed, what chance did the young trickster have? They completely ignored him and went back to mourning their father, as they were sure he would soon pass on to whatever afterlife awaited him. Only Ochossi, the god of the forest and the hunt, spoke to Eleggua as he left to look for a cure.

"My brother, your search is foolish," Ochossi said. "We have scoured all the forests, rivers, plains, deserts, and seas, and found no cure for our Baba. What makes you think you will find the answer when none of us could?"

Eleggua smiled broadly, a sight that inspired much discomfort in Ochossi's mind.

"I will find the answer," Eleggua said, "because I will look where the rest of you would never lower yourselves to look. And I will find the cure there." And with that, he took his leave.

Eleggua went to the garbage dump outside the kingdom—a place all the other spirits were too proud to visit. But the trickster god, in his guise of Eshu Beleke, the small and terrible owner of refuse and cast-offs, felt right at home there. He walked slowly through the squalor and stench, stopping only to chew the remains of a decaying rat. He dug through piles of maloderous trash, uncovering strange herbs and hidden mushrooms that thrived in the smelly wet muck, selecting one here or two there and putting them into the jute bag he carried until it was full.

Eleggua returned to the bedside of Olodumare and began to crush and mix the contents of his bag in a hollow gourd, releasing the Ashé and bringing the healing power of the herbs in through doorways that only he could open. He fed Olodumare the medicine and the great creator god was instantly revived and restored to glowing health. In gratitude, Olodumare gave Eleggua the keys to the universe and the power to open or close all portals and gateways.

As for Eleggua's older siblings, they never dismissed or doubted the trickster again.

Hat Trick

One day, for no particular reason, Eleggua decided to go out into the kingdom of men and cause some trouble. He put on his finest garments and his favorite hat. One side of his outfit was red while the other side was black, and his hat mirrored the color scheme in reverse. As he traveled, he came upon two men from different villages who had been the best of friends since they were children and who were as close as brothers. Eleggua passed directly between the friends, who admired his fine outfit. Then he hid in the bushes and watched his plan unfold.

"Did you see that man with the beautiful red suit and that fine black hat?" the first man asked.

"No, but I did see that gentlman with the fine black suit and fancy red hat," the friend replied.

The first man chuckled and said, "You mean black hat."

"No, my color blind brother," the friend laughed loudly. "What I saw was a wonderful red hat."

"The hat was black," the first man countered. "I am not color blind. Don't be stupid."

"Stupid? I am not stupid. That hat was as black as your lieing heart," the friend yelled, gnashing his teeth and waving his fist.

"No, it wasn't," spat the first man. "It was red as the blood you'll spit when I punch out your teeth!"

And with that, the two best friends began to brawl in the street. Eleggua watched and laughed. Soon, other men from each village came to join the fight. Hours passed and men on horses came, and men with swords came, and men with bows and arrows came, and men with torches came, and women came with clubs and cooking pans, and children came with sticks and rocks. Soon, all but the two friends lay dead in the blood-covered road, and both villages burned to the ground.

On seeing this, the friends stopped fighting, and Eleggua appeared before them in all his sacred glory. The friends were dumb-struck as they surveyed his black-and-red suit and his red-and-black hat.

"You foolish mortals," the trickster said. "Look what you have done. Do you see all the destruction you have wrought? Count the women and children and men who were killed in your ridiculous fight. You who have been as brothers your entire life, you have destroyed everything and everyone you have ever loved because you could not agree to disagree upon the color of my hat. For this argument, you abandoned everything else that mattered more— your families, your children, your villages, your responsibilities. You fought like spoiled children over nothing."

The two men looked at each other, horrified, and fell to the ground clutching each other tightly and sobbing uncontrollably.

And that's how Eleggua left them, grinning from ear to ear over a well-played trick. And the friends learned a difficult lesson the hard way: Appearences can be deceiving. Sometimes we have to look beyond our own perception of reality in order to see the truth from a different perspective. And sometimes, when we can't decide who is wrong and who is right, it is best just to agree to disagree. Or get a third opinion.

PART III

Yemaya in Spiritual Practice

CHAPTER 8

Altars for Yemaya

Over the many years of my practice, I have had several altars for Yemaya—in my home, in the shops where I have worked, and in shops that I've owned. They have varied in shape and size; some were extremely elaborate while others, due to circumstances, were less so. But they always had one thing in common—they were as beautiful as I could make them. Yemaya loves the finer things in life. She is a queen, after all, and her royal tastes should always be catered to as much as possible. Of course, it's not wise to go into debt when creating her sacred space. Always stay within your budget, but get the best things you can afford.

When building your altar to the Ocean Mother, the first thing you have to decide is whether you are building a working altar or a shrine. What's the difference? A working altar needs to have enough space to accommodate your spell-casting requirements as well as your offerings to Yemaya, images, flowers, and other devotional objects. A shrine is only used to hold devotional objects and doesn't have to be big enough for spell-casting.

The main altar niche in Raven's first shop featuring the handmade statue of Lemanja.

Building Your Altar

Once you have decided whether you are building a shrine or an altar, you must select the furniture you will use as its foundation. Ideally, this should be made of wood rather than metal, and it should never be black. Opt for lighter wood stains, even though the surface will probably be covered with an altar cloth most of the time. In her surface aspects, Yemaya is not very fond of the color black; in fact, many of her aspects avoid that color altogether.

Try to find a piece of furniture that has drawers, as these will give you a place to store all the tools you need to work your magic—candles, oils, herbs, crystals, etc. Drawers, shelves, or hidden compartments in and under your altar or shrine can be invaluable, because materials tucked neatly away there will actually absorb the magical vibrations of the altar over time and become more potent. I have always sought out furniture with integral storage space for just this reason.

A lot of older furniture features intricate carvings and inlays that summon up spirits of older times. Even clawed feet and detailed pulls and handles can hold quite a bit of fascination. And let's be honest. Practicality notwithstanding, there is just something mystical about cabinets and furniture like this—like something you might find in some fabulous old sorcerer's mansion. And that's just cool.

It can be hard to find furniture like this in a modern-day furniture store, although you may be able to find reproductions. Try yard sales, or vintage and resale shops. I have always had luck in places like these. I have found some amazing altar furniture on the curb as well. Because I'm crafty, I enjoy refurbishing these old pieces and I love being able to pour my energy into them. But not everyone is crafty or artistic. If you're not crafty yourself, you probably know someone who is. Pay them to do the refurbishing or support a local small business by having them do it for you.

One of my favorite altars was made from a canvas chest of drawers that I bought at a discount store when I was about twenty years old. I took off all the drawer pulls and painted a picture of Yemaya down the front of the drawers in segments so that, when they were all closed, they formed a beautiful mural. Since the canvas was lightweight, I could carry it around easily—which I did for the next few years, until the dresser quite literally fell apart.

You can decorate the parts of the altar that will be visible if you wish, or attach shells or gems to them if you prefer. I have even laid tile mosaics on altar tops, like the tiled ancestor altar I made six or seven years ago. Beauty is the key here. But if you choose to decorate your altar, I recommend doing so after you have cleansed it. And remember: Yemaya likes excess and luxury, so, honestly, in this case, more is more. But be careful that you don't go too far over the top. You want to maintain a "classy royal vibe."

Cleansing Your Altar

Once you have chosen the furniture for your altar or shrine, it must be cleansed—preferably before decorating. This is very important, especially if you have chosen a used, vintage, or antique piece. You never know how many people may have come in contact with it over the years, or what kind of energy it may have absorbed. There is a lot of unpleasant energy out there in the world today, and you don't want to invite any of that toxicity into your sacred space. If you can, cleanse the item outside of your living space, even if that means in your garage or basement, in your back yard, or on a fire escape. This can not only help to eliminate negative energies, it can keep them from invading your home.

Practicing witches have many different ideas on how to cleanse sacred space and devotional objects. You have to be careful about what you use to do your cleansing. For instance, it is best to avoid commercially produced Florida water or other spiritual colognes, because they have an incredibly high alcohol content. Unless these liquids are diluted quite a bit with water, they can eat the finish off your altar, something you obviously don't want to have happen.

Some witches prefer to cleanse by fumigation, which is cleansing with smoke using materials like sage, palo santo, angelica root, or cleansing incense. Personally, I love the fumigation method, because it is dramatic; you can see it happening. Not all magic looks like magic, but cleansing by fumigation always looks like magic to me. Moreover, the swirling smoke sparks the imagination and helps you focus on the work that's being done. If you choose to fumigate your space, be sure to follow up by scrubbing the altar with sea salt—just salt, no water—then wipe off any residue with a clean damp white cloth.

Once your altar or shrine has been cleansed, let it rest for a few hours. Use this time to clean and prepare the room in which the altar is going to be installed. There's no point in putting a cleansed altar into a dirty space. Wash the walls with cleanser to which you have added a tea of mugwort and wormwood. This will enhance the magical or psychic/spiritual work you will perform there. If you have hardwood flooring, sprinkle a dry herb floor-sweep on it. Then come back in thirty to forty-five minutes and sweep the herbs from all the corners to the center of the room. Pick up the sweepings and cast them outside into the wind. Finally, light a white or blue candle in each of the four corners of the room and pray a prayer for harmony and cleansing.

You are now ready to install your altar. Place it reverently in the sacred space you have created and say a final prayer or blessing over it to dedicate it to the goddess.

Dressing Your Altar

Once your altar is installed, you must dress it. Dressing an altar, especially for Yemaya, can be an expensive undertaking because of her refined and regal tastes. But you don't have to get everything all at once. You can work at a pace that fits within your budget. I know people who can go out and spend hundreds of dollars on altar accoutrements all at once. I, however, am not one of them. Altars for Yemaya tend to evolve and grow over time, so don't go into hock trying to get everything done all at once.

Altars to Yemaya are generally covered with fine fabrics—satins, lace, or sequined cloth in glittering hues of blue and white. My altar cloths have been an ombré blue chiffon with silver sequin dots all over it. The water-like effect of the blues is very serene and calming to me. Use whatever fabric you are drawn to, but keep it in Yemaya's primary colors of blue and white. Patterns and prints are okay; just buy the finest fabric you can reasonably afford. Let Big Mama guide you, and trust your inner voice when making a selection.

Two things you will want to acquire right away are a beautiful goblet or chalice to hold Yemaya's salted water and some kind of representation of her. Before I found an authentic chalkware statue of the goddess from Brazil, I used a mermaid figurine as a simple and affordable solution. It was a far cry from the pearl-and-shell-encrusted icons I have now, but these came much later. You can also use graphic art as a representation. A beautiful picture in a nice frame works well, or you can even use a large conch shell. And be sure to place fresh flowers on the altar or shrine every Friday.

The goblet or chalice can be either clear or blue glass. If all you can find is a metal vessel, it must have a silver hue, not gold, as gold belongs to Oshun. And it is important to change the salted water every day. Otherwise Yemaya will consider it offensive and won't drink it. This is especially true if the salt has been left to crystalize up and over the walls of the goblet, which often happens unless the water is changed daily. Salt crystals can grow and accumulate in a very short period of time. Although it may be interesting to watch this happen, it won't win you any points with Yemaya.

Your altar should eventually be equipped with a few candle holders or a large glass or ceramic tray on which to burn multiple candles at one time. It should also hold a fan. This can be either white or blue, and can be made of fabric or feathers—particularly peacock feathers (Yemaya ruled them before Oshun) or duck down (remember Kuekueye). Sea fans—flat thin formations of coral that resemble a hand fan—or the fins of a fish also work, if you can find one that is decently preserved and not extremely fragile. Seashells are also often used to adorn Yemaya's shrines and altars, as well as sand dollars and starfish. You can even incorporate decorative fish net into your design.

Finally, you will need a large white, blue, or silver platter on which to put food offerings. The shrine in my shop in Rhode Island has two tiers, with side tables and columns on either side. And just about every workable bit of space is occupied by candles, statues, offerings, and whatever else Yemaya calls for.

If you use a traditional double-edged metal athame (a consecrated ritual knife) in your work, do not place it on an altar to Yemaya. Metal blades are taboo to her and will be considered a great insult, if not a threat—one she will not take lightly. I know someone who made that mistake and now has a lovely scar on his hand to show for it. He laid a metal blade on her altar and, the moment he picked it up a week or so later, he immediately cut his hand diagonally from bottom to top. Generally, only bamboo or ceramic knives are used on an altar to the goddess or to cut her offerings.

You may be moved to hang beautiful curtains behind your altar or shrine, or a fabulous tapestry or even a painting. Some use tin art from Haiti (buy responsibly, please). If your choice pleases Yemaya, you will know it; if it doesn't, you will know that as well. Decorations hung around her altar tend to fall off the wall or get broken when she does not like them. Objects made of glass will crack; flowers may die instantly. These are all signs of rejection. Moreover, you will be able to feel psychically whether she is pleased with your gifts or not. Although this sensation is difficult to explain, it is unmistakeable. You may find yourself drawn to objects, flowers, or trinkets when you're not even thinking about offerings. If you find yourself thinking "Yemaya would like this," that is almost always a sure sign that she is asking for the item in question.

In many traditions, devotees place offerings on the floor in front of their altars, rather than on top of them. If that isn't possible—because of small children, or animals, or just because you are uneasy about attracting vermin—place them on the altar if there is space enough, or put them on a small table that is shorter than the altar and placed in front of it. This is what I do at the shrine in my shop, because leaving offerings on the floor presents a trip-and-fall hazard and my insurance does not cover acts of coconuts and watermelon. Use your best judgment here.

I don't put the usual four quarter candles to represent the elementals on my altar, although many do. This is a matter of choice. If it is a part of your tradition or your personal preference, by all means go ahead. When I do use them, I put them on four plaster columns in the four corners of the room, based on the direction the altar faces. You can keep a beta fish (Siamese fighting fish often seen in beautiful or pearlescent shades of blue) or goldfish on the altar—not only as a representation of the goddess' children, but also of life itself. If you keep anything live (even a plant) on the altar, however, don't forget to take care of it. There is nothing sacred or holy about letting a small creature slowly starve to death. You can even create a symbolic ocean for your altar. I give you instructions for this in chapter 11.

Be sure to keep the area around your sacred space uncluttered and tidy. Although I have been guilty of sometimes neglecting to do this, I am always striving to be more conscientious. Yemaya is not fond of disorder or unkempt spaces.

Put all your creativity, love, and attention to detail into the decorating and dressing of Yemaya's altar and space. Think opulence, elegance, and extravagance, and you will surely build a beautiful and pleasing environment for your spiritual work and her place in it. But always keep in mind Yemaya's legendary temper and her taboos in every decision you make regarding her altar and the tools you place on it. Color, material—it all matters. This altar or shrine will become the focal point of your daily prayers, meditations, and devotions, and of your conversations with the goddess. In fact, it becomes Yemaya's throne.

Praying at Your Altar

Praying at your altar should be a daily act of devotion. I recommend that you do this in the morning before you do anything else—even before you drink your first cup of coffee. Now, I know what you're thinking. But discipline is important. Performing your daily act of devotion before doing anything else each day can be seen as a form of sacrifice. But if it is absolutely impossible for you to do this, perform your prayers in the evening. Just make sure you change the water in Yemaya's goblet first thing each morning.

There are an untold number of prayers to Yemaya, and you can always create your own. Here are a couple of prayers I wrote to use in my own daily practice. Of course, you should always feel free to modify them for your own devotions.

Glorious mother of life,
Siren of the salt sea,

I come before you in adoration
Seeking your blessings on my life.
Queen of the white roses,
Grant me your guidance.
Bathe me in your healing waters.
Help me to walk with compassion for my brothers and
   sisters.
Keep me safe in my travels from accidents, illness, and evil.
Owner of my heart,
Let me feel you beside me
As I sing your praises.

———————————————

Omio Yemaya,
There is no limit to your power.
You who existed before creation,
You who became Queen of earth, moon, and sea,
You who are the Mother of All Life,
You who can heal all sorrow,
You who can ease all depression,
You who sees the truth of my heart,
You who protects my life,
You who brings the bounty of the sea
To bestow upon your faithful,
You who wears the rainbow as your crown,
You who are the saint of the sea
Scattering pearls as you walk upon the waves,
Giver of wealth,
Giver of life,
Mistress of the tides,
I pay you homage today
And every day to come.

Mafere fun Yemaya.
Ashé Yemaya,
Yemaya be praised.

———————————

Yemoja,
Star of the Sea,
Ruler of the inner tides,
Queen of dreams,
Compassionate Thrice-Crowned,
Be with me this day.
Watch over my family and friends.
Heal this world.
Wash clean the illness and decay of this planet.
Flood the deserts of hate.
Turn the tides of violence.
Protect those who cannot protect themselves.
Give shelter to those with no home.
Provide for the hungry.
Watch over the children.
Bring back the peace you brought to the world
When you first stepped foot upon it.
Bring back harmony.
Bathe us in your radiant love.
Mermaid of the lunar oceans,
Keep us in your heart
Today,
Tomorrow,
Always.
Ashé.

———————————

Iemanja Yemaya.

Yemaya is the Mother of Fish; her children are numberless.

Yemaya is the Mother of Life; her power is limitless.

Yemaya is the Mother of Compassion; her love is endless.

Yemaya is the Queen of the Sea; her kingdom is boundless.

In the deepest depths, her secrets are unknowable.

Where the sunlight passes through the waves, no darkness can prevail.

Where the moonlight dances on the waves, her magic is unstoppable.

Hail Thrice-Crowned Queen.

Hail Mother of Fishes.

Salve Iemanja.

This next prayer is the complete version of the traditional African chant "Kai Kai Kai Yemaya." It is meant to be sung with a lead voice and a chorus in a call-and-response fashion. It talks about Yemaya as Mother and provider, the spirit of renewal as well as the owner of rivers. Parts of this chant can be found in ceremonial videos online if you wish to learn them, but I have never seen the entire chant performed anywhere but in celebrations.

Lead voice:
Yemaya o ago oko yo Yemaya
Kai kai kai Yemaya olodo kai kai kai Assessu Olodo
Yemaya Assessu Assessu Yemaya Yemaya Assessu Assessu Yemaya
Yemaya olodo olodo Yemaya Ataramawa
Yemaya olodo olodo Yemaya Yemaya olodo

Chorus:
Yemaya Assessu Assessu Yemaya
Yemaya Assessu Assessu Yemaya
Yemaya olodo olodo Yemaya

Lead voice:
Ataramawa iya omio
Yemaya Assessu Assessu Yemaya
Yemaya Assessu Assessu Yemaya
Yemaya olodo olodo Yemaya
Yemaya olodo olodo Yemaya

Chorus:
Yemaya Assessu Assessu Yemaya
Yemaya Assessu Assessu Yemaya
Yemaya olodo olodo Yemaya
Yemaya olodo olodo Yemaya

Lead voice:
Soku ta ni wo awa Assessu
Ewi ma sere ero

Chorus:
Soku ta ni wo awa Assessu
Ewi ma sere eronide

Lead voice:
Bara ago ago Yemaya
Bara ago oro mi

Chorus:
Bara ago ago Yemaya

Bara ago oro mi

Lead voice:
Bara ago ago Yemaya
Bara ago oro mi

Chorus:
Bara ago ago Yemaya
Bara ago oro mi

Lead voice:
Omo de omo titi eyo
Eleyo la de

Chorus:
Olomo de omo titi eyo
Eleyo la de

Lead voice:
Omolo de omo ifa fakenu
Eleyo la de

Chorus:
Omo de omo titi eyo
Eleyo la de

Lead voice:
Oluba chikini oluba
Oluba chikini oluba
Ero an pipo ole yan ya o omi o lo mi omo ode

Chorus:
Oluba chikini oluba
Oluba chikini oluba
Ero an pipo ole yan ya o
A la modanse

Lead Voice:
Yemaya chikini

Chorus:
A la modanse

Lead voice:
Yemaya chikini

Chorus:
A la modanse

Lead voice:
Yemaya chikini

Chorus:
A la modanse

Lead voice:
Yemaya olodo awa lodo omi
Yemaya olodo awa lodo omi

Chorus:
Yemaya olodo awa lodo omi
Yemaya olodo awa lodo omi

Lead voice:
Yemaya alogona

Chorus:
Palo mio palo viejo

Lead voice:
Yemaya chikini

Chorus:
A la modanse

Lead voice:
Yemaya olodo awa lodo omi o
Yemaya olodo awa lodo omi o

Chorus:
Yemaya olodo awa lodo omi o
Yemaya olodo awa lodo omi o

Lead voice:
Yemaya agolona

Chorus:
Palo mio palo viejo

Lead voice:
Yemaya agolona

Chorus:
Palo mio palo viejo

Lead voice:

Yemaya agolona

Chorus:

Palo mio palo viejo

Lead voice:

Yemaya agolona

Chorus:

Palo mio palo viejo

Lead voice:

Umbo Ashé o oche umo era o
Umbo Ashé o oche umo era o

Chorus:

Umbo Ashé o oche umo era o
Umbo Ashé o oche umo era o

The following two songs are among my favorite songs for the Queen of the Sea. They were originally composed in Portuguese, but I have given you the English translations as well. I've heard them performed by many choirs, artists, and musicians, and have sung them in countless celebrations in my family. You can find performances of them in ceremonial videos online if you want to learn how to sing them in their original form.

Mãe d'agua rainha das ondas sereia do mar mãe d'agua
Seu canto e bonito quando tem luar (repeat)
Coo é lindo o canto de iemanjá faz até o pescador
Chorar quem escuta a mãe d'agua cantar vai com ela pro
  fondo do mar!

Vai com ela pro fondo do mar!
Iemanjá! Ieee iemanjá!
Rainha das ondas sereia do mar!
Rainha das ondas sereia do mar!

———————————

Mother of water
You're singing and beautiful when you have moonlight
    (repeat)
How beautiful the corner of Iemanjá
Makes the fisherman cry
Who listens to the mother of water sing.
Go with her to the depths of the sea!
Go with her to the depths of the sea!
Yemanjá!
Ieee iemanjá!
Queen of the waves, mermaid of the sea!
Queen of the waves, mermaid of the sea!

This song for Iemanja is from the Umbanda tradition.

Hoje! Hoje eu vou cantar!
Vou louvar na areia, em lua cheia a mãe Iemanjá!
Rosa do mar Minha estrela do céu azul,
Não é historia de pescador
Que o meu amor, eu vou lhe entregar Deixa!
Deixa as ondas do mar passar
Ouça o canto da bela Odoiá Oxalá
Quem mandou Um grande amor
Do fundo do mar.

———————————

Today! Today, I'm going to sing!
I will praise in the sand, at full moon, the mother Iemanjá!

Rose of the sea,
My blue sky star,
It's not a fisherman's story
That my love I will give you.
He leaves! Let the waves of the sea pass.
Hear the song of the beautiful Odoiá.
I wish he sent
A big love
From the bottom of the sea.

CHAPTER 9

Yemaya's Apothecary

Most herbs associated with the element of water are said to belong to Yemaya. Some, like the white rose, are closely associated with her, while others do not appear to have specific uses under the Ocean Mother's direction. More often than not, however, the herbs associated with Yemaya possess some specific core uses in common. They are typically found in many recipes and formulas for fertility, harmony, peace, protection, rebirth, and cleansing.

In this chapter, I have focused on plants that are generally accessible to American readers, rather than exotic plants that, while associated with Yemaya, are often virtually impossible to find or are just not available in the West. Although it is incomplete, this list will help you when you are preparing offerings for Yemaya and working spells.

In addition, many of the botanicals listed here became associated with Yemaya following her arrival in the Western hemisphere and derive from African diaspora traditions. Not all traditions share the same botanical associations with Yemaya and this is also true in Africa, which has its own botanical associations. As is true with virtually every spiritual tradition around the world, there will be debate among devotees as to which are the primary plants associated with a deity or saint. This list reflects my choices and my use of these plants in my own devotions. Feel free to adapt it for your own purposes.

- Allspice (*Pimenta dioica*)—used in spells meant to attract luck and money. Allspice is also very good for tension, stress, anxiety, and relaxation. This spice has associations with many of the orishas and is used in many of my family's recipes for oils and incense.

- Almond (*Prunus dulcis*)—purity and wisdom. The nut is used in fertility charms to ensure conception, in glamor spells, and to enhance beauty. The leaves are used in financial magic. All parts of the tree—flowers, oil, leaf, and nut—have magical uses and, when combined, can be used in magic to help with addictions. Almond oil is the carrier oil in most of my Yemaya oils. This plant is special to Yemaya for its ability to heal and for its potency in fertility rites.

- Angelica (*Angelica spp.*)—a useful and very powerful spell-breaker. Its root is used to bless and purify, and to protect people and places against harmful energies, and negative magic, spirits, and people. Angelica also amplifies female strength and power. It is particularly good for protection of the home and loved ones, and for keeping the bond between mother and child strong.

- Anise (*Pimpinella anisum*)—delicious-smelling, star-shaped seed pod that softens the heart of those who judge you and opens you up to love. It is also used to protect people from the Evil Eye and to increase psychic abilities.

- Balm of Gilead (*Populus gileadensis*)—helps ease the sorrow of a broken heart or spurned love; brings peace of mind. The healing properties of this bud connect it to Yemaya. It is an antibacterial, antifungal, and expectorant. It also has minor analgesic attributes. Balms made from this herb are good for healing minor skin abrasions and cuts.

- Calamus (*Acorus calamus*)—plant whose root and oil are used to attract love and romance. It is also very useful in domination work and spell-breaking, and it carries some healing properties as well. It is useful in treating ulcers, gastrointestinal problems, and heartburn. It also has some usefulness in the treatment of rheumatoid arthritis, and has a sedative effect. Whatever the medical purpose, it should be used sparingly and only after determining the proper dosage.

- Camphor (*Cinnamonum camphora*)—an extremely aromatic resin. Camphor is a very popular and powerful ingredient in purification rituals, cleansings, and protection spells. It amplifies psychic abilities, especially those that revolve around the seeing of visions and magical dream work, like dream-walking spells.

- Carnation (*Dianthus caryophyllus*)—softly scented flower of friendship and love. It promotes inner as well as outer peace and tranquility. Its aroma eases sorrow and depression and can lift the spirits and elevate emotions and moods. Carnation is associated with rebirth and can be used in philters and charms concerning beauty.

- Citron (*Citrus medica*)—citrus fruit that is invaluable in cleansing and purifying magic and rituals. Its cheery scent can inspire happiness and joy. This energizing fruit is great when used in solar magical workings.

- Cumin (*Cuminum cyminum*)—believed to bring good luck. This spice has been long associated with faithfulness and fidelity. It is burned for protection from the Evil Eye, as well as for deterring thieves. Brides carry it on their wedding day to ensure a happy and protected marriage. It has many uses in medical treatments—for instance, for cancer—and can help to regulate and maintain healthy blood sugar and cholesterol levels. Cumin can fight off parasites and even help as an antidiarrheal.

- Eucalyptus (*Eucalyptus globulus*)—also known as the gum tree. This tree, with its unusual bark, is among the most widely recognized trees in the world and is also among the most widely used therapeutically. It is used universally in magic that has to do with healing. Its vapors are particularly good for clearing the sinuses and throat, which makes it a great help during cold-and-flu season. It is also very valuable to singers and orators. Eucalyptus is used in purifying and cleansing rituals and can help soothe worry. Most eucalyptus species are indigenous to Australia, although a few types exist naturally in other areas as well.

- Gardenia (*Gardenia spp.*)—flower made fashionable by the late great blues goddess, Billie Holiday, and certainly one of my favorites. This beautiful, fragrant white blossom lends itself well to healing work and spells for love and happiness. Its scent inspires peace and attracts bright spirits that can aid you in your magical workings. It represents refinement and luxury.

- Grains of paradise (*Amomum meleguetta*)—also known as Guinea pepper. This plant is actually more closely related to ginger, although the association with pepper is ancient. Pliny, the first-century Roman author and naturalist, called it African pepper (and by pepper, he meant black pepper, not chili peppers). These fiery seeds are used to heat up work. They are tiny potent plant allies that can amplify and speed up all magic. Carried by many practitioners for protection and good luck, they are particularly favored by Hoodoo and Root workers.

- Jasmine (*Jasminum spp.*)—one of the most often used botanicals in my shop. The exotic beauty of this flower helps to bring abundance, inspire joy, and boost attraction. Jasmine also lends itself wonderfully to healing and lunar work. Jasmine is often used in love spells and when working on psychic development, especially prophetic dreaming.

- Lemon (*Citrus limonum*)—another bright and sunny citrus widely used across traditions and cultures for purifying and cleansing spells. Another popular use is in healing emotional hurts and heartbreak, as well as breaking our connections to toxic people. Although lemon's powers to protect inspire joy, they are also popular ingredients for spells used to "sour" relationships or situations, including to break up couples.

- Lemon balm (*Melissa officinalis*)—this lemon-scented herb has all the magical properties of the actual citrus fruit and is often added to cleansing work. Lemon balm is also a healing herb that supports emotional health and can heighten attraction.

- Lemon grass (*Cymbopogon citratus*)—Asian grass that is braided then hung up or burned in the same way that many burn sage. It protects against evil and can also remove it. It can help calm anxiety and ease depression.

- Lotus (*Nelumbo nucifera*)—considered a sacred flower around the world and across cultures. This mystical flower brings strength into troubled hearts, minds, and homes. Lotus can inspire peace and bring conflicting energies into harmony. It has long been regarded as an herb of tranquility, symbolizing wisdom as well as balance and fertility. Lotus can be used in spells concerning wealth and abundance, as well as in lunar magic and love spells. This hardy plant symbolizes strength and perseverance and the will to survive. Like the water lily, lotus is an aquatic plant whose flowers and leaves float above the water. This explains its associations with Yemaya, even beyond the transcendent beauty of the flower.

- Magnolia (*Magnolia spp.*)—one of the grandes dames of southern magical flowers. Magnolias can amplify personal power. They are associated with and used in spells regarding fidelity and faithfulness. They are also traditionally used in works concerned with gaining wisdom, ensuring freedom, and heightening feminine power.

- Meadowsweet (*Filipendula ulmaria*)—a beautiful, fluffy, clustering white flower that is used in protection work, as it inspires balance and harmony. It can also be used to attract love. Meadowsweet is very good for calming and soothing emotions and helps witches to release them. It is also an herb of love.

- Mugwort (*Artemia vulgaris*)—the primary "go to" ingredient in a lot of psychic workings, as well as for spiritual matters. When combined with the herb dittany of Crete, it can help attract and conjure spirits. Whether those spirits are positive or negative is up to the user.

- Myrrh (*Commiphora myrrha*)—a powerful purifier, making it great for protection magic. Since ancient times, the fragrant resin from this small tree has been considered holy, and was burned in temples, sanctuaries, and churches. It can help promote peace and healing. Myrrh is also widely and successfully used in spells for seduction and sensuality.

- Pennyroyal (*Mentha pulegium*)—a particularly strong herb when used for the promotion of peace and protection. It can inspire harmony and is quite a successful spell-breaker. Those who are pregnant or seeking to become so should avoid contact with this plant.

- Peony (*Paeonia spp.*)—a flower with an incredibly phallic appearance that is also one of the most beautiful and fragrant plants, making it a show-stopper in any witch's magical garden. Peony root is used in spells and rituals for protection and healing magic, and to bring strength through hard times. It increases fortitude, inspires success, and is considered to bring good luck. This unabashed flower not so subtly represents male strength and virility, and the ability to perform sexually. It can be used as a phallic substitute in spells and rituals.

- Peppermint (*Mentha piperita*)—one of the most beloved scents in my life-long work with herbs. The cheerful wintery mint is used in cleansing and purification work. When combined with any of the citruses, it becomes Fort Knox-level protection against negative vibes, spirits, and people—and at a price you can actually afford. This inexpensive plant is easily grown or found in a supermarket. It is often used for spells to help with finances and luck. Peppermint is also useful for love magic, and for fertility charms and teas. It is wonderful for improving your psychic abilities.

- Pine (*Pinus spp.*)—hardy evergreen used in spells to aid finances, as well as for purification and cleansing rituals. It is a great addition to incenses, as it smokes well and smells wonderful.

- Poppy (*Papaver spp.*)—flower that has calming properties and can be included in charm bags that help the mind. It can also be a strong ally in the struggle against addiction. To paraphrase the Wicked Witch of the West in the *Wizard of Oz*: "Poppies will make you sleeeeep." Well, kind of. The scent of poppies can help with insomnia, but the plant is more generally used in rituals of surrender and release. Some poppies also have hallucinogenic properties that can be useful on vision quests and in sacred inner work. But be careful. Not only is possession and cultivation of poppies illegal in many places, they are also a base ingredient in heroin. Using them too much can be extremely dangerous and potentially fatal—as well as illegal.

- Seaweed—acquatic botanical. The Latin binomial of its 70,000 varieties varies depending on species. Depending on the species used, seaweed can be used in magic that governs money and to establish prosperity. It is also useful in healing, and has been used for purification and cleansing. It can bring clarity to your psychic work, promote love, and assist with fertility issues. It is a very potent plant for use in banishing spells and can promote happiness and aid in works that strive to seek and/or maintain balance.

- Tuberose (*Polianthus tuberosa*)—an herb of instinct and intuition also known as queen of the night. Tuberose's fragrance helps inspire peace and can help bring about forgiveness under even the most difficult circumstances. It is also useful in purification and cleansing work, and is associated with abundance.

- Valerian (*Valeriana officinalis*)—traditionally used in healing work. This witching herb eases depression and can help elevate psychic abilities. It is useful in work centered on prophetic dreams, and inspires peace and harmony. It also helps alleviate stress, aids with grieving, and combats insomnia.

- Vetiver (*Vetiveria zizanoides*)—useful for spells and charms of attraction, as well as for protection and improving your financial situation.

- Watercress (*Nasturtium officinale*)—another aquatic plant. Because of its associations with Yemaya, watercress is used for protection when traveling in or over water.

- Water lily (*Nymphaea lotus*)—like the noble lotus, this flower inspires peace. It is used for cleansing, as well as for magic that concerns spiritual matters. Water lilies cool anger and ease depression, and they are useful in healing work and to inspire creativity.

- White rose (*Rosa spp.*)—Yemaya's favorite flower. In fact, she is often referred to as the Princess or Queen of the White Rose. This is why it is always best to offer her fresh white roses, and to adorn her altar spaces with them whenever you can. The white rose is the symbol of purity and is used in magic that encourages loyalty and stimulates self-worth. In the Victorian Language of Flowers, which assigned symbolism and phrases to specific plants so that emotions could be expressed and messages delivered via the gift of flowers, the phrase associated with the white rose is "I am worthy"—of what is for you to determine. White roses are useful in the manifestation of abundance and also help with clearing emotions and energies. They are said to promote healing. The scent of white roses also inspires romance and mystery, and, most important, the love of self.

- White sandalwood (*Santalum album*)—an exotic-smelling wood that always conjures up memories of my earliest experiences with magic and brings me right back to the beginning. Traditionally, this "master" plant is used for protection magic, as well as for love and healing work, and in spells concerning spiritual matters. (A master herb is a plant that can be substituted for any other herb because of its myriad associations and polymorphic nature. Roses are another example of a master herb.)

Fresh Herbs vs Dried Herbs

Unquestionably, fresh herbs are packed with more Ashé—the spiritual force within all natural objects and elements—than dried herbs. Whenever even remotely possible, I use fresh plants, even if that means I have to go on a nature hike or to the nursery or even to the grocery store. Dried herbs can be excessively old and bereft of any real benefit. In fact, we have no way of knowing how old herbs that are dried, crushed, and packaged for sale are. The expiration date on the packaging for dried herbs found in stores is only relevant to their use as a seasoning. If you do have to use dried herbs in your devotional practices, make sure to double the amount of fresh herbs called for and always try to make sure that the person selling those herbs actually knows how old they are—or at least how long they have been on the shelf. Independent purveyors of herbs may be more knowledgeable about their products than supermarket employees.

The Ashé in dried plants does not last forever and definitely fades with time. If the magical herb in question is more than six to eight months old, I advise against using it. It would be a shame to go through a complicated magical herbal preparation, only to find it powerless. Here's a helpful guide for determining the viability of an herb:

- Flowers and petals—three to four months

- Leaves and buds—up to six months

- Bark and wood—one to two years

- Roots—up to three years

- Seeds and pods (ungerminated)—indefinitely

Be sure to store your herbs—dried or fresh—in glass, not plastic, and out of heat and direct sunlight.

Amber jars are costly but very effective for storing and protecting your herbs, as are cobalt-blue jars. But even clear mason jars can work well if they are kept out of direct sunlight and away from heat sources. I have used all of these containers and, in all honesty, I have found very little difference in their effectiveness. The same holds true for the storage of any essential oils you may harvest from your herbs. Remember: Just because colored glass jars cost more doesn't mean that they are necessarily better than clear glass containers that are stored properly.

Crystals and Gemstones

Along with the many botanical and herbal associations that can support your devotional practices, Yemaya is also associated with a number of stones and gems. Here is a partial list of crystals and gemstones that I, personally, have found resonate with and attune to Yemaya's energy. Not all of them are traditional. As always, use what works best in your own practice.

- Abalone—a shimmering, swirling, color-shifting shell that is a gleaming example of the sea goddess' handiwork. While technically not a gem or stone, this shell is frequently used in smoke-cleansing rituals. It is associated with compassion and is a psychic conductor that promotes peace, love, and calm. Abalone helps us find the inner strength and fortitude to carry us through the most challenging and difficult times. I also find that abalone carries a purifying vibration of its own.

- Aquamarine—probably the most obvious choice on this list. This dreamy blue crystal literally means "water of the sea." Aquamarine expands and encourages acceptance and tolerance; it brings clarity to thoughts and words, and calms stressful situations and anxiety. It is called the "stone of surrender" because it helps us learn to move with the flow rather than struggling or fighting against it.

- Azurite—a royal-blue guardian stone that protects and brings great healing powers with it. It is also associated with spiritual awareness and higher thinking.

- Blue argonite—highly conductive stone energetically. This blue beauty calms scattered emotions and can help us learn patience.

- Blue-lace agate—a delicate blue-and-white variety of agate. It is a stone of self-expression, both vocally and artistically. When we lack tranquility, blue-lace agate reassures us, calms us, and soothes our fears. Like all agates, it carries healing properties as well.

- Blue topaz—the stone of forgiveness and success. Honesty, truth, and wisdom are all words that can be used to describe this glowing sparkling gemstone.

- Coral—the once-living embodiment of immortal wisdom. Coral can help you find balance. It has long been associated with royalty and wealth. Coral has healing properties that generally focus on the skeletal and circulatory systems.

- Lapis lazuli—the stone of Nirvana, sacred in many cultures and regarded as a gift from the gods. This deep-blue stone is flecked with golden pyrite, and is considered a stone of spiritual truth, love, loyalty, and inner strength. It also reveals and uncovers lies and deception.

- Larimar—often called the stone of Atlantis. This beautiful blue stone is found only in the Caribbean. It is considered a stone of manifestation and can help pull your goals and dreams into the physical world. Larimar radiates great cosmic love energy and helps to heal the throat, heart, and third-eye chakras. Larimar inspires spiritual peace and harmony.

- Mother of pearl—high-luster nacre used as inlays in jewelry, furniture, and other beautiful objects. But its value is far deeper than that. Mother of pearl helps us change and adapt as needed to navigate the stormy seas of our lives. It grants intuition and protection to those who wear it.

It works to balance emotional states and helps to increase sensitivity.

- Opal—an ever-changing stone that reflects dazzling flashes of fiery colors. Because of this changeability, opal is associated with all of the elements and enhances all magical workings. The stone itself, which consists of between 20 and 25 percent water trapped between thin sheets of hydros silicone dioxide, has a rather dubious history in folklore and was considered to be an unlucky stone by witches in the Middle Ages. Opals were said to be able to predict a witch's death, and it was also believed that the stones lost their color upon the death of a witch. They came to be associated with the number 13 and are given as gifts on thirteenth wedding anniversaries. Opal can increase the energy flow of anything with which it comes into contact. It makes a wonderful scrying stone and can raise the personal spiritual power of those who wear it.

- Opalite—a glass made from volcanic ash. This stone is controversial for a lot of snobby (sorry, not sorry) New Agers and modern witches, because most commercially available opalite is simply opalized glass. Natural opalite, however, is made from volcanic ash in which tiny particles of silicon dioxide stack up on top of each other in a pyramidal configuration that results in the cats-eye effect that appears when the glass is cut and polished. Natural opalite is olive green in color and similar in basic structure and composition to lower-quality gem opals. The two are not the same, however, and should not be weighed against each other or compared. Natural opalite enhances sexual activity and drive, acts as a mood stabilizer, and can help balance depression and anxiety. It is also a stone of communication that can help guide us through complicated transitions. Opalite carries a high frequency that calms and intrigues us with a soft siren song of energy that attracts people who are sensitive to crystal vibrations.

- Pearls (fresh-water and salt-water)—the ultimate stone of the Ocean Mother. The most powerful attribute of the glowing pearl is its ability to absorb and store energy and emotions. This means that, if you're happy, angry, or sad when you are wearing pearls, the pearls will create a record of that mood and hold it permanently within until cleansed. For centuries and across more cultures than I can list, pearls have been associated with high morality and the virtues of purity, loyalty, and truthfulness. They are also protective, which is why when we are shocked or offended, we say that we "clutch our pearls"— as a form of protection from the negativity or vulgarity of the situation. Pearls can balance energy and are associated with extravagant wealth and with piety.

- Quartz crystal (clear)—the polymorphic master healer. We call clear quartz a master stone because, like master herbs, it can do or become anything and take the place of any other unavailable crystal. Clear quartz crystals have all the magical properties you could ever really need, and far more than I can even begin to list. They clear radiation, eliminate toxins, repair and strengthen human and animal immune systems, and can relieve heartburn, acid reflux, and vertigo. They bring clarity of mind and thought; they transmute light into electrical energy, and kinetic energy (friction) into light. Try taking two clear quartz crystals of equal sides into a completely dark room and wait a few minutes until your eyes adjust. Then rub the crystals together along their flat facets as hard and as fast as you can. The stones will build up a charge and light up from within for a few seconds to a few minutes. In this case, size truly does not matter, because the smallest quartz crystal can emit, transmute, or hold the same amount of energy as the largest.

- White labradorite (blue moonstone)—a whitish, almost-clear stone with an icy-blue flash. This stone, which is sometimes called a rainbow moonstone, is not really a moonstone at all. It is a stone of creativity and compassion. Wearing it can help bring your energy into balance and harmony by diffusing it and redistributing it throughout your aura. It can enhance psychic abilities and grant visions to those who wear or carry it.

Other Associations

Here is a general list of other common associations for Yemaya that you will find valuable in your practice:

- Color—blue and all its various shades and hues. Different blues belong to different aspects of Yemaya, along with white and crystal. Red and green are also added into some of her beaded necklaces for different aspects of the goddess.

- Day of the week—Friday and/or Saturday, depending on traditions.

- Feast days—New Year's Eve and September 7, which corresponds to the Nativity of Mary, a major Marian feast.

- Metal—lead. There is a common misconception that Yemaya is associated with silver because of its mystical association with the moon and lunar goddesses. But lead is the only metal that is not corroded by seawater, so all of Yemaya's tools are cast in lead. She will accept offerings of silver, however, like coins and jewelry.

- Month—September.

- Number—7 and its multiples.

- Sacred necklace—seven white beads followed by seven blue beads, then white and blue single beads alternating seven times until the necklace is long enough to go over your head. Clear beads may be substituted for the white beads. Each path of Yemaya has a different color pallet and pattern for the necklaces. The one above is the generally accepted and most commonly found that is readily available to the general public.

- Saint—Mary, the Blessed Mother, in her manifestations as Our Lady of Regla, also known as the Black Madonna of Regla, as well as the Stella Maris, which is Latin for "star of the sea."

CHAPTER 10

Offerings to Yemaya

Yemaya will accept and value many different types of offerings, depending on the the aspect of the goddess to whom you are appealing. Perfumes, jewelry, combs, mirrors, images and statues of mermaids, statues of herself, strings of fresh-water and salt-water pearls, and corals make appropriate offerings, as do sea fans, seashells, white stones from the beach, starfish, and seahorses. Blue or white lace fans, blue or white feathered fans, and fans made of duck feathers may find favor, as well as duck feathers themselves, peacock or swan feathers, and dove or goose feathers. Other favorites include cobalt-blue glass, sea glass, tiny silver bells, fish netting, pirate flags, aquamarine, ambergris, blue and white beads, crystal beads, name-brand light cigarettes, masks, and snakes. But perhaps Yemaya's favorite offerings are of flowers and food.

Floral Offerings

It is widely believed that Yemaya values only white roses as floral offerings. While it is true that these are her favorite flower, however,

Offerings of white roses for Yemaya

this is a misconception. Yemaya loves any white or blue flowers, and accepts as offerings blossoms of all colors—white, pink, blue, yellow, red, or violet. What matters to the goddess most is the freshness and beauty of the flowers. And you should try to offer them in multiples of seven whenever possible. If you have ever ventured out to the shoreline and seen beautiful flowers floating on the waves, you can rest assured that someone has been there before you and made an offering to the Ocean Mother. Never pick them up, even if they wash up on the shore.

When presenting flowers to Yemaya at the seaside, wear white if possible. Stand with the water just covering your feet; don't venture deeper into the water than that. Hold the flowers close to your heart and pray to the goddess. Count seven waves from the end of the prayer, then toss the flowers out into the sea. Then wait seven heart beats and take seven steps backward before turning your back to the sea to show proper respect to the goddess. After all, we do not turn our backs on queens until they give us leave to go.

You can make nonfloral offerings at the seashore as well. Just make sure that whatever you put into the waves is not toxic to the sea. Strings of pearls, food items, mirrors, and combs have minimal, if any, impact on the environment. The same is true of coins. And be sure that you unwrap any flowers or cakes you offer up. It would be foolish to pollute the kingdom of the sea while asking its queen to watch over you.

Food Offerings

Practitioners make food offerings to the orishas and the ancestors to keep them nourished and strong. These offerings are usually left on or before the spirits' altars for a predetermined amount of time.

Small food offerings to Yemaya, on the other hand, are traditionally made at the ocean. If you don't have access to the sea, you can also offer up food to the goddess in a lake or pond. Or you can place your offerings in a river for Oshun to bring to the sea. Remember: Yemaya reigns over *all* water. If none of these methods are available to you, you can place your offerings at the roots of the oldest biggest tree you can find. Just be sure to clean up after yourself. We must all consider the environment when we leave food somewhere outside where it can rot and have a negative impact on the land or its inhabitants. In fact, the spirits won't be offended by it even if you have to responsibly and respectfully dispose of your offering in the trash.

Yemaya has some very specific favorite foods that she enjoys. These include duck, ram, goose, rooster, swan, turtle, guinea hen, lamb, seafood, shellfish (all of which should be cooked before given), and pork rinds. Fresh fried rinds are always best, but the ones found in bodegas and international grocery aisles are a reliable alternative. Vegetarian offerings to the goddess include lettuce, watercress, blueberries, cantaloupe, honey dew melon, watermelon, plantains, banana chips, and seaweed.

Yemaya also loves sumptuous, decadent deserts made with rich heavy creams and syrups. Some favorites include pound cake, fancy sweets, cane syrup, molasses, champagne, salt-water taffy, and white wine. Yemaya does not watch her waistline; she loves her curves. (She loves yours, too).

Cooking for Yemaya

Cooking for Yemaya is one of the best ways to show your love for her and your gratitude for her blessings. In fact, most of her children are quite skilled in the culinary arts. We cook for her in the same way that we cook for our loved ones to mark special occasions, holidays, and birthdays. Cooking for the goddess is an act of devotion and love. What we cook for her is shared with our physical and our spiritual families, and with friends. But only *after* Yemaya has been given her portion.

While each devotee develops his or her own recipes to offer to the goddess, here are a few of my favorite dishes to cook for her.

SPICY SEAFOOD STEW

This is a recipe for a delicious spicy seafood stew that is fit for the Ocean Mother. You can also add scallops to this stew, or include them with the shrimp.

You will need:

½ stick salted butter
1 red onion, diced
1 red pepper, chopped
1 yellow pepper, chopped
1 green pepper, chopped
1 lb. prepared raw shrimp (shelled, cleaned, and deveined)
½ lb. mussels
½ lb. little-neck clams
1 tbs. all-purpose flour
Salt and pepper to taste
4 tbs. minced garlic
½ cup fish stock
5 or 6 ounces oysters, shucked (canned is okay if that's
    what you have)
1 tsp. plus one pinch of good Cajun seasoning

To make the roux, or sauce, melt the butter in a large pan. When the butter is melted, add the onions and cook until they are translucent, so you can almost see through them. When the onions are ready, add the flour and mix well. When the roux is golden, add ½ cup of fish stock and stir until it boils. Then add the diced vegetables, the Cajun seasoning, and the minced garlic to the pan.

Cook for about 8 to 10 minutes, or until the peppers are nice and soft. Once they're all good and tender, add the oysters and cook another 5 to 6 minutes, then add the mussels and the clams. When they open fully, drop in the shrimp and continue to cook, just until they turn pink and start to curl.

COCONUT MACAROONS

These are not the fancy French pasteries some may think of, but rather sticky sweet mounds of coconut that have the same name. These make an incredible dessert that is appreciated by many of the orishas. It's easy to buy sweet treats to offer, but baking them yourself is an act of devotion and makes a perfect offering. And these are super easy for even the most novice baker to make at home.

You will need:

3 large egg whites (freeze the yolks to save for another dish)
½ cup sugar or sugar substitute (I'm diabetic, so I use a
    baking substitute)
½ tsp. vanilla
⅛ tsp. salt
14 ounces sweetened coconut

Preheat the oven to 325 degrees. While the oven is heating up, mix the egg whites, salt, sugar, and vanilla together until well blended and then fold in the shredded coconut.

Use a melon-baller or tablespoon to scoop out the batter and shape it into little mountains. Bake on a lined cookie sheet for 20 to 25 minutes, or until the edges are golden brown. And voilá—there you have it.

COCONUT SHRIMP

This is easily one of my favorite recipes for Yemaya, and for me as well. This is a little more difficult than some, so if you're unsure of your kitchen skills, take a deep breath, center, and go slowly. Or even ask a friend to help. These fragrant treasures will transport you to Caribbean beaches in no time flat.

You will need:

⅓ cup flour
½ tsp. salt
¾ cup panko-style breadcrumbs (I have used cracker crumbs as well, because the breadcrumbs can make the crust too hard)
½ tsp. black pepper
1 cup sweetened, shredded coconut (I use unsweetened coconut and add sugar substitute)
2 large eggs
Vegetable oil
1 lb. large shrimp

First, peel the shrimp and remove the veins, leaving the tails intact. In one bowl, sift the flour, salt, and pepper together. In a separate bowl, beat the two large eggs. In yet another bowl, mix the breadcrumbs (or cracker crumbs) with the sweetened shredded coconut.

One at a time, take each peeled deveined shrimp and roll it in the flour. Then, holding it by the tail, dredge it in the egg. Finally, coat the shrimp in the breadcrumb-and-coconut mixture, pressing on more coconut if you think you need to.

Put just enough oil in the frying pan or skillet to coat the bottom. Fry the shrimp about five at a time on medium heat for 2 minutes, then flip and fry for another 2 minutes. Remove the cooked shrimp from the oil and drain well on a paper towel. Put the finished coconut shrimp on Yemaya's offering plate and set it on or in front of her altar.

Now go make another batch for you and your family, or your coven. And then make one for me. No. For real. I'm serious. Please?

PAN-SEARED MAKO SHARK

This delicious seafood steak speaks to the warrior aspects of Yemaya. Mako sharks are the fastest-swimming sharks in the sea, as well as one of the fiercest predators. It is therefore no surprise that aspects of Yemaya like Okoto, Okunté, Achaba, and Ibu Agana love it. This is quite a simple recipe that you can easily adapt to your own needs. I know just the name makes it seem intimidating, but trust me—it is not.

You will need:

1 to 2 lbs. Mako shark steaks
Salt
Pepper
Olive oil

First, coat the bottom of a large frying pan or skillet with the olive oil and heat the pan for about 4 to 5 minutes on low to medium heat. Then turn the heat up to high.

Rub a little oil onto the shark steak and season it with the salt and pepper, then cook for 3 to 4 minutes on each side. Do not over-cook, which you will be tempted to do. Remember, well-done fish is not done well at all. Serve to Yemaya on a bed of banana leaves or lettuce with a few fried banana chips.

You can serve this dish with any number of sauces or sides. I find the warrior Yemayas like it just like this.

Tools and Sacred Objects

Food offerings for the goddess are cooked in the appropriate pan, pot, or oven, and then served (if they are smaller) on the inverted lid of a *sopera*, which is Spanish for "tureen." Beautifully decorated soperas are sacred ritual tools in Santeria and other African Traditional Religions. Each orisha has a dedicated tureen that is decorated in a manner that is unique to the spirit (see below). The only time the food touches the sopera, however, is after it is cooked and placed on top of the sopera lid, which is flipped upside down to receive it.

The sopera for Yemaya is traditionally a white ceramic soup tureen decorated with blue designs. Yemaya's tools live within her tureen, which also serves as the receptacle of her Ashé. I have seen unbelievably ornate soperas that are blue and adorned with porcelain mermaids and roses. I've also seen soperas decorated with clay masks of Yemaya.

Below you'll find a list of sacred ritual objects that symbolize the various traits of the orishas. These are similar to talismans or power objects used in magic—like athames, wands, and chalices. In most traditions, when someone is initiated, they receive Yemaya's tools or emblems cast in lead. These can be used as a focus for sympathetic magic or to channel the specific aspect of Yemaya's Ashé needed to manifest. Not all traditions necessarily use exactly the same symbols for the same purposes, or to represent the same spirit, however. The list given here is just the most commonly accepted one.

- Anchor—symbol of stability

- Cowrie shells—tools for divination, usually found in groups of eighteen

- Full moon—symbol of Yemaya's status as Mother of the World

- Half moon—symbol of Yemaya's wisdom and esoteric knowledge

- Seven silver hoops or bracelets—symbols of Yemaya's wealth and status

- Life preserver—emblem of Yemaya's influence and desire to come to the rescue of her children

- Mermaid—siren representing Yemaya's supernatural beauty

- *muneca* (Spanish word for "doll")—figure holding a serpent (*acaro*) and a mask (*samgagua*) that represents the two spirits that live within Yemaya in her aspect of Yemaya Olokun—the two primal forces of the oceans to nurture or extinguish life

- Oars—shown in pairs to represent the good and evil that lives in all mankind and the need to keep them in balance

- Otains—seven smooth black stones gathered from the seashore

- Ship's rudder—symbolizing Yemaya's influence and power to keep us on the right path

- Sun—emblem of the power of life and Yemaya's power to extinguish it

Meditation

Meditation can be another way to offer your devotion to the goddess. In fact, meditation has become an especially important part of my own spiritual practice. It helps me ground my energy and recharge my batteries, so to speak. It also enables me to commune with Yemaya and other spirits in a calm and peaceful way, which in turn allows for clearer communication.

If you are unfamiliar with meditation, I suggest using the "rainbow method" of relaxation. Sit comfortably in a chair. Do not lie down, or you will probably find yourself falling asleep. Clear your mind and begin to take slow deep breaths. As you do this, focus on the rhythm of the rise and fall of your chest. Listen to your heartbeat, and synchronize your breathing to the pulse of your beating heart.

In your mind's eye, see and focus on the color red and begin to relax. Let the color change to orange as you relax further. Next, see or imagine the orange turn to yellow and then to green. Relax more deeply with each shifting hue. Allow the green to become blue and then indigo. You are feeling weightless now and at peace with the universe. As you see the indigo color transition into violet you are completely immersed in what we refer to as the "alpha state," the deepest level of consciousness before sleep.

It is here that magic begins for most witches and spiritual practioners. When in alpha state, you cannot make mistakes or do anything wrong. In fact, everything you do will be on point and flawless. Allow your consciousness to remain bathed in the violet glow for a little while and prepare yourself to take a little trip to visit the queen of the living waters, Yemaya.

You are standing at the seashore. The sky is a clear robin's-egg blue. The sun shining down on the golden sand makes it feel warm beneath your feet. A gentle breeze caresses your body with the scent of salt water. The ocean is calm and crystal blue. The light glitters like diamonds along the surface, as you begin to step into the water and walk farther and farther away from the shore, until you are totally submerged. You can easily breathe here and feel no threat of drowning. Your legs grow fins and you begin to swim downward into the depths of the ocean. You are greeted by schools of brightly colored fish that swim around you. You continue to swim until you arrive at a magnificent palace made of living coral and gleaming mother of pearl. The large door is open and there is a softly glowing light within the royal palace of the Ocean Mother that beckons you to enter.

As you swim into the palace, you see many sirens and merfolk lingering in the hall. They smile at you as you swim by. They are beautiful creatures with flowing hair and glistening skin. Their tails are sleek and powerful, and their fins are an explosion of color and light. They point you toward the royal throne room. The way is guarded by two mermen holding tridents who ask you why you are there. Answer them honestly and from your heart. They unblock the way for you.

You enter.

In the center of the room, on a throne of shells, she sits. Her ebony skin shines in the soft light, her long dark hair floating freely all around her. Her flowing gown seems to be made of the water itself. Her dark eyes are kind as she focuses them on you; her smile is warm and inviting. Immediately, you feel welcomed and at home, as if you have been there your whole life. She extends her arm and opens her hand, inviting you to come closer.

When you are just in front of her, she takes both of your hands with a mother's touch. You feel her maternal love for you as she begins to speak. She welcomes you to her kingdom and into her home. She asks you why you have sought her out, just as the guards did. Answer truthfully and from the heart. She begins to speak again, offering you permission to ask her what you really want to know. Make your request, and then listen to what she has to say. The reply will go much deeper than a simple answer to your question.

She begins to give you guidance and advice. Pay attention, because she does not repeat herself and you may lose the valuable information she is giving you. Listen for as long as she continues to speak. When she has finished, she tells you it is time to return to the surface world and presses a large white pearl into your hand. She kisses you gently on the top of your head and sends you on your way home.

As you begin to swim back up from the ocean depths toward the surface, you begin to see the rainbow materialize in reverse. Violet—you are becoming slightly more aware of the physical world. Then the light changes to indigo and then to blue as you rise higher and become more aware. The blue turns to green and then to yellow—you can sense the physical realm. Yellow becomes orange and then turns to red, at which time you are returned to your full consciousness.

Write down any important information or guidance you received. What did you tell the guardians? What did you tell Yemaya? What was her advice to you? How did all this make you feel? What does the pearl Yemaya gave you mean to you?

CHAPTER 11

Invoking Yemaya

Because Yemaya was given dominion over all aspects of Olodumare's power, she can perform any type of magic. Traditionally, there are two main types of magic commonly practiced—spells and ebbos. These are similar, but not the same. An ebbo is a major formal offering or work that calls on the intercession and influence of a specific orisha. When performing an ebbo, we borrow Ashé from a spirit when our own may not be sufficient to provoke the response we are seeking. Ebbos are used more widely in times of urgency and great need. They are generally performed for seven days, after which their remains are disposed of in the ocean. If you don't have access to the ocean, you can give the leftovers to a river and let Oshun bring them to the sea—to Yemaya—or place them under the tallest oldest tree you know, or even place them in the trash and ask Eleggua Beleke, the owner of refuse and cast-offs, to accept them.

When you perform an ebbo, you make a formal offering to a spirit that consists of its favorite things. In a sense, ebbos are sacrifices that don't actually involve sacrificial victims like chicken or fish that are slaughtered as part of the working. By contrast, the offering up of an actual sacrificial victim releases Ashé all at once, in a single moment, and that is a lot of power to channel. Personally, I reserve that kind of working for extremely serious needs.

Although many people view this kind of animal sacrifice as brutal or negative, this is a misunderstanding of the practice. In fact, sacrificial victims are always skinned, cleaned, butchered, cooked, and eaten by the community, unless they are being sacrificed to cure an illness. Before the working, they are pampered, honored, fed well, and ceremonially prepared for a holy purpose. Surely this is preferable to being kept in a pen, fed garbage, killed without honor, and sent out in forms that no longer even vaguely resemble their previous being.

An animal that is sacrificed and shared with the community gives its life for a noble cause. The victims of KFC do not. Today, we no longer have the same relationship with our food that we once had. We have been removed from the ancient processes of husbandry and the chase. In the old days, if you were not willing to hunt prey and prepare it yourself, or raise livestock and slaughter it yourself, you did not eat. While this may sound cruel by 20th-century standards, in fact it is not. No matter where you buy your meat, someone killed it for you.

Unlike ebbos, spells are performed without the influence of the divinity. They are cast by calling on the magician's own Ashé and the Ashé of herbs and stones and other natural substances associated with a spirit or the result sought by the working.

Recipes, Spells, and Ebbos

In this section, you will find some of my favorite recipes, spells, and ebbos (major formal offerings). As always, the more personal your practice is, the stronger it will be. So please feel free to adapt any of these workings to your own goals and purposes.

YEMAYA CLEANSING WATER

This is a recipe I have made and sold in my shop for years. It makes a rather large batch, but keeps well in the fridge or out of heat and sunlight. I love making this with friends and students, because it can be a serious bonding experience. You can quite literally smell and feel the magic swirling around you in the air. All my memories of brewing up this potent potion are filled with happiness—and perhaps more than a little raucous cackling. Oh, and tequila.

You will need:

1 block camphor
1 large bunch fresh peppermint or 2 drams of essential oil
2 drams neroli essential oil
2 drams sweet orange essential oil
2 drams citron essential oil
½ cup whole cloves
2 drams lemon grass essential oil
Peels and juice of 3 lemons
10 cinnamon sticks
1 to 2 oz. rose petals
1 ½ oz. jasmine blossoms
2 drams bergamot essential oil
1 handful of lavender
2 liters of vodka or perfumer's alcohol
1 gallon water
1 blue and 1 white candle
Billie Holiday CD—optional, but why wouldn't you want
    that voice to bless your work?
Containers and jars
1 to 2 yards clean unbleached muslin or cheesecloth
1 large and 1 small stock pot or a three-quart saucepan

Wooden spoon
Strainer

I also recommend having a shot of tequila handy, although this is optional. It will help ground you when the atmosphere becomes flooded with the psychic energy of this concoction and you start to trip. (It happens. Not always, but it *does* happen.) A nice dry wine can help as well, as can good coffee, tea, soda, or fruit juice for those who avoid alcohol. The sugar and/or caffeine in these beverages can also help ground your energy.

First, before you begin your work, call upon Eleggua to open the doors of power to you and bless your work. I suggest writing your own prayer for this, but here is a relatively simple one you can use:

Eleggua keeper of the keys,
I ask you to open the roads to the Spirits,
And bless this work.
Maferefun Eleggua,
Ashé Eleggua!

Once you have called on Eleggua, invoke the spirit whose influence you wish to have on your work, if there is one. In this case, we are making this water under the auspices of Yemaya, so compose a small prayer or use one of the ones found in chapter 8.

At this point, you can turn on the Billie Holiday CD and light the candles. Get yourself into a peaceful and calm mindset. Remember that what you're creating is going to reflect whatever feelings you're having, so don't bring any low vibrations into the work space. Next, gather all of your tools and ingredients in your kitchen or wherever you're going to do this work.

Put the large stock pot on the back burner of the stove, but don't turn it on yet. Place all your botanicals (flowers, herbs, and sticks) on a double layer of the fabric and tie it up into a bundle. Fill the small pan about ¾ full with alcohol and set it to simmer on a low heat. Place the fabric bundle in it and simmer the bundle for about an hour, adding a little water to the mix as needed. The resulting liquid will be a dark reddish color and heavily perfumed.

When the bundle is ready, squeeze all the extra juice from it using the wooden spoon. Pour it all through a strainer lined with the rest of the fabric into the large pot and add the remaining alcohol. Simmer the bundle in water a second time for 30 minutes and squeeze out the fluid again. Strain whatever juices remain into the previous batch. Be sure that you never use the wooden spoon for anything else, because you will never get all of the Yemaya water out of it.

Bring the stock pot to the front of the stove and simmer on very low heat. Shave the camphor block into the liquid, stirring it occasionally and letting it dissolve. While it simmers, take a shot of tequila or a sip of wine or coffee or other beverage and relax. If you are not using fresh peppermint, add the essential oil now. And be careful not to let the pot boil.

Once the camphor is dissolved, add each of the essential oils and the lemon juice and stir with the wooden spoon. Simmer another 15 to 20 minutes and cool. Strain the liquid into containers, filling them about ½ full, then top off with distilled or purified water. Seal and shake well.

Two things happen when you perform this working: Your house will smell like paradise, and you'll have a stockpile of one of the strongest spiritual cleansers you'll ever use.

EBBO TO SECURE A NEW HOME

Performing this ebbo is an easy and reliable way to call down blessings and ensure security when you move to a new home.

You will need:

1 platter
1 blue pillar candle
Yemaya oil (see below)
Yemaya incense (see below)
An image or statue of Yemaya (a printed photograph
    works, but you can even use a large shell to represent
    her)
Sardines—any brand or flavor will do
7 cakes or other sweet pastries
7 silver coins
7 plantains or bananas
Roasted seaweed
1 can coconut cream (not water, not milk)
White flowers
1 chalice
The home's address written on clean white paper, along
    with the name of the landlord or current owner
An offering for Eleggua to open the way to Yemaya (candy,
    cigars, rum, or jutia—roasted possum and fish ground
    together and available as a powder-like substance in
    most botanicas)

Make your offering to Eleggua using the prayer above, or compose one yourself. Then gather all of your spell components and prepare and bless your ritual space in your usual manner. Dress the candle with the oil and place it on your altar.

Assemble the seven cakes or pastries in the center of the platter. In three of the corners of the platter, place the roasted seaweed, leaving the corner to the right of the pastries empty. To the right of the cakes, in the last corner, place the sardines. You can put them on a small dish or in a small bowl if they have sauce. Then place the seven silver coins over the food.

Fill the chalice ¾ full with the coconut cream and place it beside the offering on the platter, along with the plantains or bananas. Drizzle the remaining cream all over the food and place the address of your new home on top. Then pull the heads of the white flowers off the stems and place them all over the top of your offering. Set the platter at the feet of the image or statue of Yemaya and leave it on your altar for seven days. It may start to smell pretty bad, but that is part of the sacrifice. At the end of seven days, dispose of the remains in the sea or in a river.

SPELL TO SWEETEN CIRCUMSTANCES

This is hands-down the most fun—and at the same time the grossest—ritual I have ever done. And you are about to find out why.

You will need:

7 small cakes
1 can coconut water
White rum
7 white flowers
An offering for Eleggua to open the path to Yemaya

Petition Eleggua and ask him to bless this work. You can use the prayer above or compose one of your own.

For seven consecutive days, place a small cake on your altar and pour molasses over it. Each day, place a new cake on top of the old cake and add more syrup. On the seventh day, crumble all of the cakes, put them in a large pot, and pour in the can of coconut water, the tops of the seven flowers, and the white rum.

Now here's the fun part

Rub handfuls of this sweet sticky mush all over your naked body. Be present in the moment as you do this. Feel all that sweetness soaking into your skin; feel it changing your luck and outlook. Revel in the joy of covering yourself with cake! I mean, come on, when have you ever been able to do something that was this much fun? Yes, it will feel silly. And yes, it is okay to laugh. Magic does not always have to be a solemn and serious experience. Yemaya, and most of the spirits we serve, have a sense of humor. Just ask the platypus.

Spend as long as you can stand covered in this tasty muck, and then go take a shower to rinse it all off. Do not use soap or body wash until the following day. For this reason, this ritual is best performed at night before bedtime. I recommend sleeping on a separate sheet or towel to avoid sticking to your bed linens and staining them.

EBBO FOR DIVINE INTERVENTION

Need a miracle? Need Big Mamma to sweep in and snatch you out of the worst situation you have ever been in? Are you at the end of your rope, stranded with no hope in sight and no apparent way out? Then this is the offering you want to make. This ebbo is performed on the floor in front of your altar. I suggest putting a plastic mat down first.

You will need:

7 small blue taper candles
7 small white pillar candles on 7 small white plates
1 large watermelon (whole)
7 silver dimes
7 copper pennies
7 blue flags (make them with toothpicks and blue paper)
Cane syrup or molasses

7 white roses
7 seashells
7 silver bells
1 large platter
A chicken heart (you can get one at a butcher shop, supermarket, or grocery store)
A ceramic or bamboo knife
A small toy—something from a gumball machine, for
   instance

Begin by asking Eleggua to open the way and offer him a small toy in gratitude. Place the watermelon on the platter and put that on the floor. With the ceramic or bamboo knife, carve seven holes in the watermelon just big enough to insert the seven blue taper candles. Put the chicken heart in the center of them, and then stick the seven blue paper flags all over the watermelon's surface.

Cut the stems of the roses short (¼ to ½ of an inch) and use the knife to insert them into the watermelon between the flags, then balance the seven seashells on it. Let the roses and flags support them.

Pour cane syrup all over the watermelon, and then put the silver bells on it. Put the pennies in a circle around the watermelon and put the dimes on top of them. Place the white candles on the white plates and place them in a circle around the platter. Light the blue candles, then the white ones.

Pray for Yemaya to intervene on your behalf. Pray hard and with complete belief that your spiritual mother will fly to your aid. Pray until the candles go out and then leave your offering on the floor until the request is granted or it rots. Finally, dispose of the remains in the ocean or in a river.

SPELL TO STOP GOSSIP

It can sometimes be extremely helpful to know exactly who is speaking ill of you. If you do not know the culprit, just focus on an unknown gossip.

You will need:

1 large fish
1 smaller fish that can fit inside the larger fish
7 hot peppers (the hotter the better—chilis, ghost peppers, jalapenos, habaneros, scorpion peppers, or a mix of them)
Brown paper (lunch bag or craft paper)
Red ink
A curved needle
Twine or thread
Before you begin, ask Eleggua to open the path to inner power and give him a small offering.

Write the name of your tormentor (or the words "unknown gossip") on the brown paper with the red ink. Write it over and over, crossing over on top of itself until the name is completely illegible. Fold the paper until it is small enough to fit into the smaller fish's mouth.

With the curved needle, sew the fish's mouth tightly shut and knot the twine or thread seven times. Now slice open the larger fish's belly and pull out all the organs inside it. Place the small fish, along with the seven hot peppers, into the large fish and sew the belly shut. Then sew the mouth shut as well.

Take the fish out into the woods and hang it from a tree to rot. Your enemy will stop talking against you as the fish decomposes. You can also bury the fish if you prefer.

AN OCEAN FOR YOUR ALTAR

If you live far from the waters of Yemaya's kingdom, you may feel as if you are too removed from the goddess to hear or feel her properly. But you can create a miniature ocean to keep on your altar or elsewhere in your home to help strengthen your connection to the Ocean Mother.

You will need:

> 1 large glass bowl—short and wide, rather than tall and thin
> Stones from the beach
> Seashells
> Sea salt
> An appropriate anointing oil
> A blue seven-day candle in a glass jar
> A few fresh-water pearls from the craft store (or sea pearls,
> if you can afford them)
> 3 coconut candies or cookies

Wash out the bowl and dry it, then it scrub with salt. Ask Eleggua to open the door and offer him the three coconut candies or cookies as thanks. At twilight on a Friday evening, cast a magic circle or create sacred space in your usual way. Then invoke the Western spirits of water, saying:

> Though I am far from the sea spirits of the West, come
> forth
> Mermaids and undines, siren singers, daughters of Yemaya.
> Lend your power to this holy work.

Scrub the outside of the candle jar with salt and anoint it with holy oil, Yemaya oil (see below), bergamot oil, or the oil of any of Yemaya's sacred herbs (see chapter 9).

Place the blue seven-day candle in the center of the bowl and then line the bottom of the bowl with the shells and stones. Say this prayer to Yemaya as you add each shell or stone. Be mindful of what you are doing and why you are doing it.

> Yemaya, my mother, I ask for your blessing
> As I create your kingdom in my home.
> Empower this vessel and fill it with your radiant presence.
> Ashé Yemaya, Ashé.

Add the pearls and a palmful of the sea salt to the bowl and slowly fill it with water. If you have or can find a small lead or ceramic figure of a siren, you can also put that in the bowl. (Even an aquarium decoration or mermaid figure will do.) Light the candle and say a final prayer. You can use the one I give here or compose one of your own.

> Blessed Mother, I thank you for your blessings
> And acceptance of this vessel,
> Dedicated to your sacred powers.
> Yemaya be praised.

Then release the spirits of water from your circle, saying:

> Spirits of the sea, powers of water,
> I release you back to your Western realms.
> Thank you for your presence and protection this night/day.

Open your magic circle if you have cast one and burn the candle for seven hours every Friday. Clean everything in the bowl every seven days, then reassemble the miniature ocean and replace the candle when it burns out. You can also add a few silver coins if you wish. Make sure you keep up on the maintenance of your ocean; do not let it get dirty.

SEAWATER PROTECTION

This is one of my family's most potent home-protection spells.
You will need:

3 keys
7 glass mason jars,
7 quartz crystals
7 silver coins
7 bluing (anil) balls
7 cubes of camphor
7 pennies
7 silver fish hooks
Yemaya oil (see below)
Juice of 7 limes
7 blue votive candles
Holy oil
Clean white towel
Square of blue cloth

Go to the seashore on a Full Moon at high tide. You can find tide tables online or in publications like *The Old Farmer's Almanac*. Step into the water up to your ankles—go no deeper than that. Ask Eleggua to open the way and leave him three keys as an offering of thanks. Then count the next seven waves. After the seventh wave, invoke Yemaya, saying:

Queen of the Sea, mother of life,
I come to you this Full Moon night.
In the reflection of your mirror, beneath your holy gaze,
I give you honor, homage, and praise.

Wash the mason jars thoroughly, then dry them and scrub them inside and out with sea salt. Now begin to fill the jars, first adding the quartz crystal, then the silver fish hooks, then the bluing and camphor, and finally the silver coins. As you fill each jar with the talismans, center your energy, calm your mind, and focus on the work you are performing. It is very important to keep your mind clear while preparing the glass jars. As you do so, chant the following:

I call the power of the sea,
Keep my home safe and protect me.

Repeat this seven times for each group of talismans, for a total of thirty-five repetitions of the chant.

Once you have done this, fill each jar ⅔ full of seawater. Leave the seven pennies in the shallows of the sea and go home with your jars. Set the jars on small white plates in a circle on the floor that is big enough for you to sit in comfortably—you're going to be there a while. Place a blue votive candle dressed in Yemaya oil (see below) or protection oil or the essential oil of any one of Yemaya's sacred herbs on top of each lid (see chapter 9).

Take a cleansing bath with sea salt, bergamot oil, Florida water, and the juice of seven limes. Soak in this bath for 28 minutes. Not 27, not 30—but 28. Timing, in this as in all magic, is extremely important.

Pull the stopper from the tub and allow all the liquid to drain out before standing up and getting out. *Do not rinse*. Pat yourself dry with a clean white towel and put on fresh clean clothes or your ritual garb. Anoint your Third Eye, heart, hands, and feet with holy oil.

Cast a magic circle or prepare your sacred space according to your tradition. Then seat yourself within the circle of jars and light each candle one by one, while chanting:

Spirit of the sea, protect me.

When all of the anointed blue votive candles are lit, close your eyes. In your mind, see the glowing circle of water rushing like a river around you. Hold this image in your mind until you can see it when you open your eyes (or at least feel it). For the next 28 minutes, repeat this chant:

Spirit of the sea protects me from harm and evil.
I am free.

Then banish the spirits of the West, saying:

Spirits of water, I thank you for lending your Ashé to this rite.
Return to your kingdom beneath the waves.
Hail and farewell.

Close the magic circle if you have cast one. Carefully step out of the circle of glass jars and very carefully distribute them throughout your home and let the votives burn out.

Leave the jars for seven days, then strain out the talismans, reserving the liquid in a large pot or bucket. Tie the talismans up in a square of blue cloth and hang it from the highest place in your home that you can reach. At twilight on the seventh day, take the pot of liquid and pour it in a circle around your home, moving clockwise. Wash the mason jars and keep them for future use.

SIREN SPELL

Before the birth of Oshun, Yemaya was considered to be the most beautiful of all the goddesses. Even after the goddess of attraction arrived on the scene, Yemaya's regal beauty was still considered to be without equal. This ritual can help you channel the seductiveness of the mermaids, and honor your own body in all its natural beauty. This ritual is best performed naked.

You will need:

1 large scallop, clam, or tiger-paw shell deep enough to
    hold a small amount of powder

1 dried white rose
1 handful of dried jasmine flowers
1 handful of yarrow flowers
1 handful of dried seaweed
Mortar and pestle
7 white votive candles dressed in Yemaya oil (see below) or
    one of her other sacred herbal oils (see chapter 9)
Sweet-smelling incense
Pendant in the shape of a trident, mermaid, shell, fishtail,
    or ship's rudder
1 bottle of seduction, fire-of-love, come-to-me, bewitching,
    or attraction oil
1 large mirror

First, petition Eleggua to bless your working and open the door to Yemaya's power. Then cast a magic circle or prepare your sacred space in the manner to which you are accustomed, and invoke the Western spirits of water, saying:

> Spirits of the twilight waters,
> Come forth and bless the magic cast this night.

Prop the mirror up on your working altar at an angle that lets you see yourself reflected within it. Anoint the 7 white votives, set them in front of the mirror, and light them.

Charge the herbs one at a time, holding them in your hands and concentrating on what it is that you want the herbs to do in your spell. Then grind each one into a fine powder in your mortar with the pestle. Use all the strength and concentration you have. Do not cut corners here. *Do not use a coffee grinder.* Some witches may say that is okay, but I completely disagree. The whole point of grinding the herbs by hand is to imbue them with your intention and your will. You do not get this benefit when you use a mechanical tool—not to mention the fact that you should never cut *anything* for Yemaya with metal blades.

Once you have ground the herbs to a fine and smooth powder, fill the shell with as much of the powder as it can hold. Then, while watching yourself in the mirror, dust your entire body with the powder, being careful not to get any into your eyes. Hum or sing a melody to the sirens as you do this. Visualize the dust shimmering and sparkling as it caresses your skin. Feel the energy of attraction and seduction wash over you like waves. Let your skin absorb the power and vibrations. In your heart and mind, allow yourself to become one with the mermaids and sirens, then touch the pendant to your Third Eye, and say:

Thoughts of beauty now reside in my soul and in my mind.

Touch the pendant to your eyes and say:

Eyes of deepest mystery, reflect the fathoms of the sea.

Touch the pendant to your lips and say:

Sweet the words and sweet the kiss; in my mouth the taste of bliss.

Touch the pendant to your throat and say:

To my voice the siren song; my power to enchant grows strong.

Touch the pendant to your heart and say:

Let my heart beat wild and free, with the spirits of the sea.

Hold the pendant in both hands and say:

I hold the power in my hands to inspire the hearts of man/woman.

Anoint the pendant with the oil you chose and let it sit on your altar for seven nights.

Release the spirits of the West from the circle, saying:

Spirits of the Western waters,
I thank you for aiding me in this rite.
Return to your kingdom beneath the sea.
Hail and farewell.

Take a scented bath or refreshing shower to remove the powder so it doesn't clog your pores. Then give yourself a facial or indulge in some other pampering beauty routine. Wear the pendant you used in the ritual whenever you want to amp up your allure, your seductiveness, your self-confidence, or even your love of self.

SPELL TO RELEASE TROUBLES

This is one of my most treasured spells. I learned it during a very dark time in my life, and I am pretty sure it's the reason that I am still alive today. The original spell was much less complicated than the version I'm giving you here, but that's only because of the sheer amount of sorrow and desolation behind it—and I hope beyond hope that that is not the case for any of you. I developed this version shortly after casting the original spell, and I have recommended it to clients and friends for over thirty years.

This spell should be cast only in times of sorrow and pain. It is *never* to be used to make a simple request of Olokun.

You will need:

1 pearl (fresh-water or salt-water)
A needle to draw blood
Sealing wax or a small candle (sealing wax is far better
    because it forms a waterproof, air-tight seal)

A lighter or matches

Some fruit to offer Olokun (he accepts all fruits and vegetables)

1 fairly large chambered shell—a nautilus, large snail, or hermit crab shell will do (just make sure it is large enough to contain the pearl, some blood, and as many tears as you can catch within it)

3 small pieces of hard candy

Travel to the seaside when the tide is going out. When the waves are pulling away from the shore, they are energetically pulling the emotions out of you. Ask Eleggua to open the door and offer him the three small pieces of hard candy in thanks. Sit by the water's edge and contemplate your troubles, letting the water pull the emotion up from your heart.

Put the pearl into the shell. Then prick your index finger with the needle and allow a few drops of your blood to fall into the shell. Ideally, it should fall on the pearl, but if it doesn't, that's okay.

Now—and this is the most important and, for some, the hardest part—talk to Olokun and tell him in great detail of your woes. Allow all the sadness you feel to come up to the surface and let your tears flow. Do not fight them or struggle to regain your composure. This outpouring of emotions is absolutely key to the spell's success. Raise the shell to your face and allow at least seven tears to roll into the chamber. More is fine, but make sure you've left enough room to seal the shell with the wax.

Fill the shell almost to the top with sand, leaving just a little space. Light the candle or sealing wax and use it to seal the cavity shut. The sand will give the wax something to adhere to, as well as give the shell the weight that it will need in order to sink into the water.

Hold the shell to the top of your head and ask that your thoughts of sorrow be drowned. Then hold it to your eyes and ask that your tears of pain be drowned. Now touch it to your lips and ask that no more words of sorrow come from your lips.

Finally, hold the enchanted shell against your heart and pray with all the strength you have left in you that your heart may be mended and that your sorrow, pain, and desolation may be swept down to the bottom of the ocean and drowned. Really feel this. Concentrate all of your power and energy on it. Then throw the shell out into the water as far you can.

Call on Olokun to take the shell to his kingdom and hold it there forever. Then roll the fruit into the water as payment for the work, take seven steps backward, turn, and go home. Do *not* look back for any reason.

Once you are home, take a nice warm bath, put on fresh clean clothes, and go to bed. In the morning, things will look much brighter.

YEMAYA OILS

These three versatile oils can be used in spiritual perfumes, for anointing and blessing tools, and for candle dressings. The first is a blend that has been in my family for quite a long time, but it is not the one that I manufacture for my shop. That one is a family secret, for family eyes only. But I believe you will love this version as much as I do. The second and third oils below are also very powerful and versatile.

I tend to like almond oil as a base carrier oil when working a recipe for Yemaya because it's one of her preferred offerings to begin with. These recipes make one ounce each, but you can always adapt them to make a bigger batch. I recommend using only the best-quality oils you can purchase, within reason. This is definitely not the time to be cheap and use sub-par ingredients. If you think Big Mamma won't notice, you're wrong.

For this all-purpose oil, you will need:

A glass bottle or new mason jar
A small funnel
Several reusable eye-droppers
1 pearl (fresh-water or salt-water)
1 oz. almond oil
7 drops bergamot oil
2 drops rose oil
7 drops sandalwood oil
4 drops magnolia oil
2 drops lemon verbena oil
Sea-salt crystals
Alcohol for cleaning
Mortar and pestle

Pour the almond oil into the jar and let it rest a few minutes. Add the other oils in the amounts and order given above, using a fresh dropper for each one. As you finish with the droppers, place them in the alcohol to remove the oils. Crush the pearl in your mortar with the pestle, scoop out the glittering pearl dust, and add it to the oils. While praying to Yemaya, swirl the contents of the jar around for about 3 minutes. Add a small sea-salt crystal to the jar. Seal the lid and keep it on Yemaya's altar for seven to fourteen days to charge it and absorb some of her Ashé. This oil can be used for anointing yourself before any magical working that involves Yemaya.

This second oil is similar to the first, but differs in the essential oils used. It is useful for cleansing and blessing work.

To make it, you will need:

1 oz. almond oil
14 drops sandalwood oil
12 drops gardenia oil

6 drops lemon oil

2 drops peppermint oil

2 drops citron oil

1 drop white rose oil or rose oil

1 pearl (fresh-water or salt-water)

1 mason jar for mixing or another glass container that has an airtight seal

Several reusable eye-droppers

Alcohol for cleaning

Pour the almond oil into the mason jar and let it rest for a few minutes. Then, one at a time and in the order given, add each of the essential oils slowly, drop by drop. Use a fresh dropper for each one and place it in the alcohol after use to remove the oils so that it can be reused.

Crush the pearl in your mortar with the pestle, scoop out the dust with a spoon, and add it to the oil. While praying to Yemaya, swirl the oils in the jar for 4 or 5 minutes, until everything is completely blended. Seal the mason jar and charge the oil on or before Yemaya's altar for seven to fourteen days to absorb some of her Ashé.

This third Yemaya oil uses slightly different ingredients and incorporates an aquamarine crystal rather than a pearl. This oil works well in spells for healing heartache and work that calls for the power of persuasion.

To make it, you will need:

12 drops carnation oil

7 drops coconut oil

2 drops jasmine oil

3 drops star anise oil

1 small aquamarine crystal

1 oz. almond oil

Glass mason jar or other glass container that has an airtight
   seal
Several reusable eye-droppers
Alcohol for cleaning

Pour the almond oil into the mason jar and let it rest a few minutes.
Then, one by one, add the other essential oils one drop at a time and
in the order given, using a fresh dropper for each one. When finished
using them, place the eye-droppers into the alcohol to remove the oil
so you can reuse them.

While praying to Yemaya, swirl the oils around in the jar gently
for 4 to 5 minutes until they are completely combined. Drop the
small aquamarine crystal into the jar and seal it. Place the jar on or
in front of Yemaya's altar for seven to fourteen days to charge it and
absorb some of her Ashé.

YEMAYA INCENSE

You can use these two recipes to create incense that can enhance the
power of your Yemaya workings. I like to make incenses with varying
fragrances; I always think it's good to have choices.

To make the first, you will need:

Rose petals
Powdered sandalwood (if you can find it) or sandalwood
   chips
A couple of star anise pods broken into pieces
Lemon verbena
Lavender
Basil leaf
Meadowsweet
A dust mask (trust me—you will thank me later)

Mortar and pestle
Ceramic or glass bowl (copper is fine too)

Put on the dust mask and crush equal amounts of all the herbs except the star anise into a fine powder in your mortar with the pestle. Focus on Yemaya while you do this. I usually chant or sing to her while I work on this recipe. Then grind the star anise pieces separately into as fine a powder as you can. If you are using sandalwood chips, you will have to grind them separately as well.

In the ceramic or glass bowl, mix all the herb powders together and pray to Yemaya over the mixture. Place the powder on her altar or on the floor before it if there is not enough room on the altar. Leave the herbal incense there for seven to fourteen days to charge it and absorb some of Yemaya's Ashé. Store the incense in an airtight container and burn it over charcoal in your workings.

This second incense is made in the same way, but uses slightly different ingredients.

To make it, you will need:

Jasmine
White rose (or whatever color rose is available to you)
Carnation
Peony
Lemon balm
Mortar and pestle
Glass, ceramic, or copper bowl
Dust mask

Put on the dust mask and crush equal amounts of all the herbs, one at a time, to a fine dust in your mortar with the pestle. As you finish with each one, place the powder into the bowl. Mix the herbs together while praying to Yemaya. When the powders are well blended, place the bowl on or in front of Yemaya's altar to charge it and absorb some of her Ashé. Store the incense in an airtight container and burn it on charcoal to enhance your workings.

YEMAYA SHELL CANDLES

These beautiful devotional candles are very easy to make. I have not made them in many years, but while I was reading over my old recipes for this section, I came across this one and decided to share it. These always turn out beautifully and they always delight the Ocean Mother. Making them can also be a fun afternoon project for witchlings if you have them scampering about.

Votive candlewicks with an attached base are available in most craft stores in the candle-making secion. Murex shells, lion's paw or large scallop shells, cockle shells (yes I know), and clam and quahog shells all work well for these candles. Shells with thicker walls work best, because they can handle heat better than thinner shimmery shells, which will burn. Be sure that the shells you choose have absolutely no cracks or holes, and that they can stand with the open side up without tipping or rolling over, unless you plan on setting them on a base.

You will need:

Votive candlewicks
A block of wax
A double boiler
A glass measuring cup
Blue candle-wax coloring blocks
Craft glue (not hot glue) or some tack-like clay
Crushed pearls
Tiny shells
Whole pearls
Small pieces of coral

Yemaya oil (any of the three given above)
Several large deep shells

Set up all your supplies in the kitchen. Melt the wax in the double boiler. While it is melting, use the craft glue or clay to fix a wick base into each shell. The bases are thin and very malleable, so they can easily be pressed and bent to conform to the curve of the shell.

When the wax is completely melted, add the blue candle-wax coloring block and stir until it melts and the wax reaches the color you desire. Once you have achieved this color, add the Yemaya oil until you feel that the wax is scented strongly enough. Then, very carefully, pour the wax into the glass measuring cup.

Now line up your shells on a wire cooling rack that has a double layer of paper or cardboard under it. One at a time, carefully pour just enough wax to cover the base of each shell completely. When that wax is solid, slowly fill each shell with the remaining wax. Each shell should be just under completely full.

Now quickly—before the wax is set, which will not take very long unless the shells are very deep—dust the surface of the wax with the crushed pearl. Then decorate with the tiny shells or uncrushed pearls, but be sure to keep these away from the wick. Don't throw out the extra wax or pearl dust; keep them on hand. When the wax has completely hardened, there may be small divots around the wick. If so, re-melt the wax and fill them in.

Repeat this as often as necessary, sprinkling more of the pearl glitter to cover your repair work. Some people like to decorate the outside surfaces of their candles with cosmetic-grade glitter or wax shapes like shells or stars. This is fine. Use your own creativity when making these devotional votive candles.

Place the shell votive candles on or before Yemaya's altar for seven to fourteen days to charge them and absorb some of her Ashé.

Consulting the Cowries

Consulting the sacred cowrie shells has been a staple in the divination rituals of Santeria, Candomblé, Ifa, and other African-derived traditions for centuries. A detailed discussion of this very complicated and involved traditional art is too complex to give here. But I want to share a little bit about this practice so that you can consider introducing it into your devotions to Yemaya.

I generally recommend leaving such divination to professionals and to practitioners who have spent many years preparing and training to perform the rituals. But a simple way to divine with the sacred cowrie shells is to use them to ask the spirits uncomplicated yes-or-no questions. This method of divining, called *Obi,* involves using four cowrie shells. In this practice, there are five possible answers you can obtain from the four shells (see below).

To begin, you will need four opened cowrie shells—cowries that have had the natural hump on their backs cut off and sanded smooth, resulting in a fairly flat and even surface. If the cut side faces up during a reading, that shell is considered to be silent. If the side of the cowrie shell with the natural mouth-shaped opening faces up, that shell is considered to be speaking. The patterns and ratio of silent to speaking cowries deliver the simplified answers you seek. You will also need a mat or cloth that you can place on the floor or a table. This is where you will cast the shells. Before casting any shells, always say a prayer to the spirits, asking them to speak.

Hold the four cut cowrie shells in your hands and pray about the situation about which you are divining. Concentrate on nothing else and blow on the shells. Then shake the shells in your hands a couple of times and gently roll them out onto the mat. Your answers will come to you as follows:

- Four mouths speaking (all four shells landing with their natural mouth-shaped opening facing up) indicate *Alafia*. This is a blessing, so your answer is "yes." You will have more success in what you ask about than you dared to hope for. A second throw can determine how long this luck will last.

- Three mouths speaking and one mouth silent (three shells landing with their natural mouth-shaped openings facing up and one shell landing with its flat side facing up) indicate *Etawa*. This answer is less positive than *Alafia* and can be considered a strong "maybe." Although this 3-to-1 pattern is generally looked on as a "yes," the one silent shell adds an element of doubt. This answer is not stable and you will need a second throw to further explain what lies ahead of you. If the second throw yields either *Alafia* or *Ejife* (see below), the answer is "yes." If the second throw yields *Etawa* again, that indicates that you already know the answer and are being told to accept it and move on. If the second throw yields either *Okanran* or *Oyekun* (see below), the answer is "no."

- Two mouths speaking and two mouths silent (two shells landing with their natural mouth-shaped openings facing up and two shells landing with their flat sides facing up) indicate *Ejife*. This is the most positive answer possible, telling you that all is in balance—there is harmony; this is perfection. Never throw a second time when you receive this answer.

- One mouth speaking and three mouths silent (one shell landing with its natural mouth-shaped opening facing up and three shells landing with their flat sides facing up) indicate *Okanran*. This is a clear and definite "no." What you wish will not come to pass easily, if at all. You will need to do much work to change the situation.

- Four mouths silent (four shells landing with their flat sides facing up) indicate *Oyekun*. This answer portends absolute darkness and silence. It is the irrevocable "no." In fact, it is more than this. It tells you that you are surrounded by very negative forces, and that you will need to do spiritual cleansing to clear the condition in question. The dead may speak in this pattern and you may need to make a series of additional throws to learn the nature of the problems that keep you in the dark, or if the spirits are asking for specific offerings or actions on your behalf in exchange for help. Only after you have these answers will you be able to turn your attention to the original situation.

Be sure to keep your shells in a special bag or box. I suggest never letting anyone else touch them, because this can interfere with the psychic relationship you will be building with them.

Choosing Your Own Path

I hope that these few workings find a place in your heart and your spiritual practice, as they have for me and my spiritual family. Remember that magic is all around us all the time; it's natural and accessible at all times. If you choose to worship Yemaya without the practice of spells and magic, that is a totally legitimate choice. There is no rule that says you have to. You may choose to purchase your oils and incenses and candles, rather than make them yourself. Again, there is nothing wrong with that.

Remember that the worship of the orishas is a deeply personal practice. No one has the right to tell you that their way is the only way. There are so many differences from house to house in the same traditions that you will find very few identical practices. The important thing is to find your own path to the Ocean Mother and to bring her spirit and power into your own life.

Journey Home

The journey to finding Yemaya can be long and difficult if you travel it without guidance. For people outside of African Traditional Religions, it can be especially difficult to find that guidance because most of these traditions are very tight-lipped and suspicious of outsiders who want to learn their practices. Outsiders who are Caucasian have an even harder time, unless they know someone who is willing to take them on as students. Turning to the internet is not always helpful, because it is packed with inaccurate and misleading information, some of which is simply made up by people who want to appear as if they are connected to these paths, when in reality they are not.

In fact, it has never been easy to learn about mystery traditions or find authentic practitioners of these paths, especially when they do not want to be found. Most of these traditions are comprised of closely guarded secrets that are passed down in spiritual houses from generation to generation. Unfortunately, the passing down of these traditions is often accompanied by fear and suspicion, which tends to keep these cultural walls firmly in place and make them virtually impossible to breach. But sometimes, if you are lucky and persistent, you can get around them.

But when the siren calls, all must answer.

When I talk to witches and other Pagans or spiritual seekers about Yemaya, I can clearly see the fascination in their eyes. I can see the desire to know her, to learn her ways. I see that look in the eyes of customers as they stand in front of the Yemaya shrine in my shop. I see it in the eyes of all the people who come to my workshops and in the discussions about Yemaya. I see it and I recognize it, because I once carried that same look in my own eyes. As a very light-skinned person of mixed heritage myself, I probably would have wandered aimlessly for years trying to find answers had I not had relatives who were willing to teach me. Had they not taken me under their wing and brought me into their house, I probably would have fallen for every scam, every scheme, and every fraudulent group I came across.

When I first started down the path to Yemaya, I was not taken seriously. I was treated with suspicion and mistrust, like a thief who had somehow snuck into the ranks of the faithful and plotted to steal their secrets and sell them to the world. I had to study and train twice as hard to get half as far. I stumbled and failed many times and often felt as if I had no hope or chance of ever reaching the point I am at right here right now, almost thirty-five years later. But I now see my journey through different, and hopefully wiser, eyes. I see the value in surrender—something I could never have seen at seventeen, or at twenty-five, or at thirty-five for that matter. And even now, I sometimes still find myself struggling against the tide—exhausted and stuck in the same spot just treading water—rather than finding the fulfillment that surrender can provide.

I have also come to recognize the value of failure. It is said that, without failure, we would not have the determination or drive to succeed. And I certainly believe this, because I know that failing in front of those who thought me unworthy drove me even harder to prove myself and to find those who would eventually accept me and help me discover my spiritual center.

From Brazil to New Orleans to Connecticut to Rhode Island, my journey with Yemaya has taken me to places where I would never otherwise have gone. I've seen and experienced things that I never could have imagined existed outside of my once very narrow world-view. Seeing the world through the lens of my devotion to Yemaya, I have seen my inner truth—both the churning whirlpools of Olokun's rage and the peaceful calm of Assessu. I have been Okunté's sword; I have seen my arrogance mirror that of Ibu Ina. But I have also seen my compassion and love for family and friends that is inspired by Yemaya in her totality. I have been both blessed and punished for my deeds and misdeeds by the righteous Ocean Mother. And I learned. And I grew. And I survived.

With her popularity in the magical and spiritual worlds rapidly expanding, it is important to remember Yemaya's role in the universe. In her final incarnation, she becomes, quite literally, the center of it—the axis on which it all turns—devoting herself for all eternity to the care, well-being, and continued procreation of mankind. I believe firmly that she will continue to call more and more of her children to her—all races, genders, colors, shapes, and sizes—from all around the world. No one who seeks her with a truthful heart and sincere desire to serve will be denied The lines being drawn in our society and the separatism being spread by people who want to believe that they can own the goddess cannot endure. Those who believe that only they can decide who can or cannot worship at her altar will not succeed.

There are many paths to Yemaya, and none of them are exclusive. If only those who claim to have a unique and exclusive right to practice in her name would look beyond themselves, they just might see a bigger family and a bigger world in which this most beloved goddess can flourish even more than she already has.

Yemaya traveled the world with Obba Nani, goddess of domesticity and devotion, after her divorce from Shango. She went to every country in the world, leaving a part of her Ashé in all of them. Is it really so hard to imagine that people from every place she touched feel her and seek to know her? To believe they do not is pure hubris. Who are we as mortal men and women to presume we know more than the divine?

What I *do* believe is that more and more witches will incorporate Yemaya into their magic and that their lives and work will become enriched by this. I believe they will forge a stronger connection to the Mother of All Life and, through that connection, become more powerful in their work to cleanse our world and its societies. They will become better able to heal the wounds inflicted on the earth by mankind. They will learn the lessons of mercy and compassion that Yemaya teaches, as well as the ways of her warrior aspects, which will, at times, be necessary for survival.

I believe that, by spreading Yemaya's presence throughout the world, witches, Pagans, and even Christians will turn to her more and more, seeking the protection of her blue mantle. And I believe that the Ocean Mother, the great *Ye-omo-eeja*, will never turn her back on the children devoted to her.

I swear that, when I was just a child on that rock jetty in the midst of an encroaching high tide, Yemaya came to me and saved my life. As incredible as it may seem, she came to me again after I died in the horrible accident from which I never completely recovered and granted me the sight. Years later, when I was ready to die while being victimized by someone I desperately loved—someone I had thought loved me back—it was Yemaya Olokun who turned me away from a self-destructive path and taught me how to work the magic that could give me the strength to leave all of that pain and hurt and betrayal behind. She helped me stand strong in my boots and soldier on.

Yemaya spirit doll

Every time I paint a picture of the goddess or make a spirit doll in her image, every time I blend her incense or oils, every time I cook gumbo or jambalaya for my friends, every time I place flowers on her altar and sit quietly to hear her council, I remember the first time I knew that I was hers. It was the first time I ever felt that I was truly home.

APPENDIX

Index of Aspects and Spirits

- Abbata—lover of Yemaya whom she rendered deaf so he could not hear anyone ask him about her secrets. He became the lover of Inle, god of hunting and fishing, who dwells where the rivers and the sea meet, merge, and mix. Inle was once married to Yemaya, but she cut out his tongue so he could not reveal her secrets. The connection between the deaf Abbata and the mute Inle was so strong that they were eventually able to communicate psychically.

- Agayu—god of erupting volcanoes and the embodiment of all nature.

- Agwé—king of the sea in the Haitian tradition.

- Arganu—orisha who becomes Omi Leto, the axis upon which the world turns. It is in the story of Arganu that Yemaya transitions into Ibu Agana, the Mother of All Life.

- Ashé—Yoruban term for the spiritual force within all natural objects and elements.

- Babalu Ayé—god who heals the land and supports the elderly.

- Eleggua—trickster god of chance and fate, keeper of the keys to the gates between the world of mortal man and the world of the orisha. He is the spirit of communication and crossroads. Without him, nothing can happen. Eleggua facilitates or denies all communication with the other gods.

- Eshu—darker aspect of Eleggua, the trickster. Although often graphically depicted with enormous male genitalia, Eshu also contains multiple powerful and prominent female manifestations as well. His sexuality is thought to be extremely fluid.

- Ibu Achaba—the first female diviner. In this aspect, Yemaya stole the secrets of the cowrie shells from her then husband, Orunmila, the god of divination. This act of independence brought about the end of their marriage. She prefers to wear the colors turquoise, green, and yellow and only speaks to her children with her back to them. Her name means "anchor," and she is referred to as "she who comes from heaven."

- Ibu Agana—a very angry aspect of Yemaya who is married to Oko, the god of agriculture. Her name is translated as "crazy." Although blessed with a beautiful face, Ibu Agana's beauty is marred by seven cysts on her belly. One of her legs is also smaller than the other. This causes her to limp and hinders her ability to dance, which brings both shame and anger into her heart. She resides at the very bottom of the sea in Olokun's realm. Ibu Agana has ties to Oroina, whose domain is the magma of volcanoes and the cosmic radiation and heat of the sun.

- Ibu Assessu—an aspect of Yemaya who is found where the water is still and brackish and where the frothy white foam of the sea touches the dry sand. She appears clothed in sky blue as the waves crash onto the shore, and can be found where springs gush up from the earth. Do not pray to her for things urgently needed, but rather for things that need a lot of time to grow.

- Ibu Elowo—keeper of all sunken treasures lost since the beginning of time. She rules the expansiveness of the sea and all of its riches. She is often compared to a mermaid living in a treasure-filled grotto at the bottom of the ocean where no one can hope to reach her wealth.

- Ibu Mayelewo—the favored daughter of Olodumare, once married to Oko, the god of agriculture. She lives in the middle of the sea where the seven tides mingle. This aspect of the goddess is very prideful and judgmental, preferring to look at people only from the corner of her eye. She is often seen wearing a mask, carrying a serpent, and holding a fan of coral. She lives at the bottom of the sea with Olokun and often acts as his messenger. A superior businesswoman, her name means "one who loves money" and she is immensely helpful in matters of finance.

- Ibu Okoto—a fierce aspect of Yemaya who is a very formidable warrior. She is associated with the color navy and with pirates; we find her wherever blood has been shed in the water. She fights with scimitars and daggers, and, unlike most manifestations of Yemaya, she prefers to wear pants when she rides to war.

- Ibu Okunté—a furious warrior aspect of Yemaya who (in the Western hemisphere) steps out of the sea each winter bringing ice and snow. Her temper is legendary and she never forgets a slight or insult. Okunté is married to Ogun, the god of war, and lives with him in the forest. She goes into battle with machetes and wearing a chain from which hang her husband's tools. She stands just outside the gate of Olokun's kingdom and allows visitors in and out.

- Ibu Tinibu—an aspect of Yemaya who brings great crashing waves to enjoy or destroy. She lives in the crest of the highest surf and rules the tidal wave. When angry, she threatens to flood the land.

- Ikoko—orisha who has dominion over all aquatic plants.

- Inle—hunter/fisher/healer god who dwells where the rivers and the sea meet, merge, and mix. Inle thus inhabits two realms simultaneously. He also acts as the doctor or physician for the other orishas. He dresses in fine clothes and adorns himself with cowrie shells and gold beads. He has feminine features and long braids, and was once married to Yemaya, who cut out his tongue so he could not reveal her secrets. He became the lover of Abbata, whom Yemaya had rendered deaf so he could not hear anyone ask him about her secrets. Their connection was so strong that the deaf Abbata and the mute Inle were eventually able to communicate psychically. Inle is a patron of homosexuals.

- Iroko—spirit of the ceiba tree. When Yemaya fled into the forest, Iroko sheltered her within his branches for days until her hiding place was revealed by Kuekueye the duck.

- La Sirène—Haitian *lwa* (spirit) of the ocean who appears as a beautiful and bewitching mermaid. She rules over music, the arts, beauty, and magic. Her sacred number is 7 and her colors are pale green, white, and pink. She teaches sorcery to humankind by taking them with her under the sea for seven years. *La Baleine*, the whale, is her shadow self. She is married to Admiral Agwé, the king of the sea.

- Logunede—god of transitions. He is the son of Oshun, goddess of love and attraction, and Ochossi, god of archery. He spends half the year dressed as a woman and half dressed as a man. He has become popular as the patron of transgendered and bisexual people as well as drag queens.

- Mami Wata—not one specific spirit, but rather a term for all the African water-spirit families. In modern times, the title has been anthropomorphized as a single water goddess.

- Nana Buruku—goddess of the moon, also known as "Grandmother Wicked." In some traditions, she existed before all other things, even Olodumare. In others, she came into being following the rape of Yembo by Ogun. Yembo's rage was so great that she split into two distinct entities: Yemaya, who became the oceans, and Nana Buruku, who ascended to the heavens, where, hidden from sight, she watches over mankind in the light of her silver moonbeams. Her temper is horrible and dangerous, and her punishments are doled out swiftly and without mercy, but her love is just as prodigious.

- Obatala—Father of the World and once husband to Yemaya. Obatala promised Olokun that Oko, the god of agriculture, would not reject him. Oko's ultimate rejection set Olokun on a path of hatred and mistrust against the surface world.

- Obba—goddess of domesticity and devotion. Obba was the first wife of Shango, god of thunder, lightning, and fire. She is the goddess of marriage and was the first teacher.

- Obi—divination techique that involves casting four cowrie shells to obtain five possible answers to yes-or-no questions, depending on how the shells land when cast.

- Ochossi—god of archery and hunting. He fishes with Inle, god of hunting and fishing, and they are very close friends. He is also considered to be the long arm of the law, because, when he hunts, no one can escape him.

- Ochumare—rainbow serpent and the patron of artists, gay men, Lesbian women, and transgendered people. He is the movement of energy and light, as well as the ruler over seasonal changes and cycles. His symbol is the rainbow, now a major LGBTQ symbol that also appears as Yemaya's crown. Seen as half human and half serpent, he is also the embodiment of transformative energy.

- Oddua—the female aspect of Obatala.

- Ogun—god of war, iron, and progress. Though he raped Yembo, the first incarnation of Yemaya, she later married and then abandoned him.

- Oko—god of agriculture. His affair with Olokun, the force of primal sexuality, held serious repercussions for mankind.

- Olodumare—supreme creator god considered to be the Father of All Life, as Yemaya is considered the Mother of All Life. After Olodumare created the earth, gathering up all the dust and particles of matter in the universe, he created a vast hole into which he poured the remaining gasses accumulated during the creation of the planet. These became the oceans from which Yemaya was born. He is one third of the divine triad and reigns over honesty, purity, and oaths. Slow to anger, he is the epitome of the loving father figure.

- Olokun—an aspect of Yemaya who rose as a humanoid figure from the ocean depths after Olodumare created them. He rules over the deepest parts of the ocean—the deep dark, where no light penetrates. He had a homosexual relationship with Oko, the god of agriculture, and is thought to be very gender fluid. Often pictured in contrasting images as very masculine or androgynous, he represents the primal sexuality of the ocean and its place in the LGBTQ community.

- Olona—orisha who lives in Yemaya's lakes and protects them from harm and the pollution of mankind.

- Olose—orisha who rules over lagoons. Crocodiles are her servants and some traditions depict her as being married to Olokun.

- Omi Leto—the axis upon which the world turns. Literally "Mother of the world."

- Ony Ocuny—Yemaya's title as Queen of Queens or High Queen over all other "orisha queens."

- Orula, or Orunmila—god of prophecy and divination. Once married to Yemaya, he divorced her for stealing the secrets of the cowrie shells, which are used as a divination tool in Yorubaland in the manner that runes, coins, or yarrow stalks are used in other divinatory systems. It has been said that he left Yemaya to have a homosexual relationship with Ogun, the god of iron and progress, although in many traditions, he is said to be very homophobic, and will not initiate gay men as priests.

- Oshun—goddess of love and attraction, and the youngest orisha. She was given dominion over rivers and waterfalls by her sister, Yemaya. Oshun often chooses to ride (possess) male priests and accepts all demonstrations of love and sexuality. She has a strong homosexual following.

- Oya—goddess of the wind and storms. She spits fire and throws lightning, skills she stole from her husband, Shango, the god of thunder, lightning, and fire. Depicted as a fierce warrior, she accompanies Shango into battle wearing pants and a false beard, so she has become an informal patron of Lesbian women. She is the goddess of universal change and rules over the air, the marketplace, and the cemetery.

- Pomba Gira—the singular name for a large family of spirits who rule over sexual deviance, death, magic, prostitution, burlesque performers, and outcasts. In some traditions, they are considered a female incarnation of Eleggua, the trickster. They are matrons of women and gay men.

- Shango (Chango in Santeria)—god of thunder, lightning, and fire. Shango is Yemaya's foster son, and she is the only orisha he fears. He rules over male beauty, sexuality, and virility. Although he has a reputation as a great womanizer, he is syncretized with Santa Barbara, the young virginal female saint. It has been said that Shango and Eleggua shared such an afinity as to be of one heart.

- Yemaya Atarawa—easily the wealthiest avatar of the goddess. She is the owner of all the riches of earth and sea. Though her home is in the depths, she guards the coastline where plants and grasses grow wild.

- Yemaya Ibualaro—aspect of the goddess who, in some traditions, rules over life and death. That to which she gives birth she can also take back. Her whim decides who survives and who perishes at sea.

- Yemaya Ibu—aspect of the goddess who lives with her sister Oshun in the rivers and goes on land only to meet with her lover, Agayu, the spirit of the volcano.

- Yemaya Ibuina—queen of tragedy and conflict. This aspect of Yemaya is known for her harsh attitude, her blunt demeanor, and her tendency to be forward. She never sugarcoats anything she says, regardless of the arguments or even wars (which she loves) her words may cause.

- Yemaya Ogunosomi—sister of Okunté who lives on the surface of the water and has a fondness for mountains. This warrior aspect of Yemaya accompanies Shángo, god of thunder, lightning, and fire, and Ogun, god of war and iron, into battle with two machetes. She is very beloved for her ability to heal the sick.

- Yemaya Oro—the singing mermaid. She lives with the dead of the sea—the drowned and the shipwrecked—and reigns over them. She is mysterious and stays hidden.

- Yembo/Yemmu—mother of all orishas and cosmic mother of all life as we know it. Yembo emerged from the sea spray after Olokun rose from the ocean depths and gave birth to the stars, the moon, and the sun. Her kingdom is the regions where the light of the sun and moon penetrate the darkness of the sea. After Olodumare placed the souls in each orisha, she delivered them into physical bodies. She is the true crown of Yemaya and the first incarnation of the goddess.

- Yewa—once the favorite daughter of Obatala, Father of the World. After Shango, god of thunder, lightning, and fire, disgraced her, she became the embodiment of decay.

ACKNOWLEDGMENTS

I want to thank my devoted husband, Malcolm Anderson, for his continued love and support, as well as my late sister and brother, and my godson, Charles White. I am also grateful to all the priests who taught me what kind of priest *not* to be. I give heartfelt thanks to everyone who ever said I was too white, or not brown enough, or not black enough—everyone on both sides of my heritage who said I couldn't, shouldn't, and wouldn't. Because, you see, I *have*. You made me study harder, fight longer, get stronger, and rise above it all. And I thank my late parents with all my heart for adopting me after I was abandoned. I hope I've made you proud, and I wish you were here to see me finish something impossible.

Thank you as well to all those who have walked this road before me and all those who will walk it after me. Thank you, Stevie Nicks, for being the constant soundtrack of my life and as I wrote this book. Special thanks to my best friend and spiritual "brotha from anotha motha," Rob Mack, for never not believing in me, for pushing me to create every day, and for supporting me in so many ways. You saved my life. I won't forget. JT, thanks for everything. Alexandra, Christopher, and Pamela, thanks for helping me keep the shop going as I dedicated myself to this writing. Thank you, Judika Illes, for believing I had, and for helping me find, my own voice. And finally, I thank my ancestors, both known and unknown.

TO OUR READERS

ABOUT THE AUTHOR

A spiritual artist who has dedicated his life and work to the service of the great mother goddess, Yemaya, **Raven Morgaine** is a practitioner of Candomblé, New Orleans Voodoo, Santeria, and witchcraft. He is the owner of the Familiar Spirits shop in Coventry, Rhode Island, where he creates and sells the spirit altar dolls for which he is renowned. Raven's art is on display at the Wonder Woman Museum in Connecticut, and he has been featured in numerous publications and podcasts. He lives in Rhode Island. Follow him on Instagram @ravenmorgaine.